The path to Nothing

Marcel van Heijzen

Dedication

To those that put me on the path of "Nothing".

Books by the Same Author

Beating Cancer

Spiritual Development

Short Stories

The Life of Derek

My Life as a Lioness

A Life of Adversary

The Path

A Seekers Guide

Life's Surprises

The Alternative

The Penguin that wished it could Fly.

Acknowledgements

This book came about because some friends questioned the existence of real guru's in the material world. They commented because the people they met up to now did not make much of an impression; they meant nothing. I started with analysing "Nothing" as a concept, and the result is this book. I am eternally grateful to be handed the challenge to think about "Nothing".

I also like to thank my friend Brian and my son Eelco for their input when creating this book.

When anybody would like to discuss subjects out of this book, please get in touch. I am always available for those that need contact or assistance.

To get in contact, please, write an e-mail to:

Marcel.vanheijzen@yahoo.co.uk

You can also register on my website to receive my weekly blog.

https://alyaconsultancy.com/

The writing of this book started in December 2020.

Copyright of this book rests with Marcel van Heijzen.

All parts of this book may be copied and used, provided reference is made to the author.

Image by kamalpreet singh from Pixabay

Contents

Introduction 10
What this book intends to achieve 17
Consciousness 28
An analysis of the mind 37
Personalities 48
Preparation for the Path 59
The Concept of Karma 67
The Concept of Communication 75
Coincidences 84
Spiritual Experiences 93
The Astral level of Awareness 103
The Audible Lifestream 110
Proceeding on the Path 120
The behaviour of an Initiate 130
The Physical 143
Liberation from Matter 153
The Spiritual Region 161
The Masters 169
The Nameless 180
The art of Meditation 187
References 199
About the author 200
About this book 201

Introduction

This book is a sequential write up; it follows my previous book, The Alternative. However, it dives a lot deeper into the various subjects we discussed in that book. After an initial discussion with somebody and further discussions with others, I started this analysis. My initial contact told me that he looked at many spiritual leaders and found nothing of interest. His statement triggered me on the subject, and I asked him to think about the concept of "Nothing". I also evaluated the issue, and I wrote a short story and one of my blogs about the subject. The resulting questions led me to write this book.

Although I use the term "Nothing", it is my way of indicating that our scientists miss something when they do not investigate anything they cannot detect. Sufficient literature is on the market from spiritual leaders to justify some investigation in the concept of what we refer to as our consciousness. Scientific studies are available, but I did not find many references to spiritual literature. It appears that we still hesitate to mix science with spiritual belief systems.

In a way, I understand this hesitation. Many systems have as a base a belief in a spiritual leader who has long since passed away. However, as applies to a lot of mud, one can find gems when looking properly.

-o0o-

My whole life, I worked as an engineer in various jobs around the world. During my life as an expatriate, a lot of events happened that we class as coincidences. Although the chances that events like these happen are small, life is like this, and I gave these situations no thought.

After contracting serious cancer and being told that I had four months to live, my thinking and approach to life changed. Via my family, I contacted somebody who told me he could cure me – which the medical establishment told me was not possible. I had to go on a vegan diet and reduce sugar intake as much as possible. My organs got measured for imbalance, and this doctor found a lot of defects. To sort this out, I needed to add food supplements to my diet. He also established that pesticides saturated my body. A few more food supplements sorted this out, while all fruit and vegetables we ate needed washing in water with a bit of brown vinegar. It took about four years for all the cancer symptoms to disappear completely, but these life changes resulted in me still being alive after six years, and my cancer appears gone. My body is a lot healthier; I hardly contract a cold, I have not had the flu for a long time, and various other defects appear gone. The balancing of my organs initiated this change, supplemented by my change in lifestyle.

In addition to the recommended change, the challenge I faced brought me to think about my way of living. Other people around me passed away; why did I survive? With assistance from a friend, I got introduced to Ishwar Puri and the spiritual teachings he brings worldwide. Being introduced to spirituality changed my life. After I decided to retire, I felt that engineering was no longer my vocation, and I started writing. I used my investigative skills as an engineer to dive into the subject of spirituality, and this study got me to where I am at present.

I am not a guru, and I do not want to be such a person. I write about spirituality and subjects related to human development. I class myself as a seeker. During the last few years, my life changed again; I stopped smoking and drinking, and I eat mainly a plant-based diet, which some refer to as vegan. At times I allow little non-vegan treats in my life, but nothing related to meat.

This year 2020, Christmas was a party we had with the two of us during the lock-down, so I got persuaded to eat a nice salmon steak with an Eton Mess as dessert. Eating this was not a problem for me. I regard the path I follow as essential. However, holding to any direction without caring for other people's feelings is also, in my view, not correct. We go through the lockdown without too much trouble because we both give in to each other's quirks and strong feelings. I will deal with the why of my diet later in this book.

What I write about in this book is not what I accomplished. I am on the path, and by studying what I may find, I hope one day to experience such events. A seeker should not advertise spiritual progress, and my readers should, therefore, not confuse my writing with my progress on the spiritual path. My task is to follow the seeker's way, and it is my belief that I must assist anybody who asks. I do this by writing and studying spirituality. People contact me, and I do my utmost to help. I write to translate what I learn into a language that I hope many people can understand. I do this because I found that often spiritual writings are difficult to comprehend.

People told me that my writing is easy to understand. Possibly this is because of my limited intelligence and the use of a second language. Anything I do related to spirituality is for free. I do not believe in earning money by assisting people; in my view, that means I start a business. My present-day activities relate to the challenge I went through; making money out of this is not my objective. Having made the previous point, my books are in various libraries globally, and my wife laughs when I inform her that I have another income from my books. Up to now, it amounts to about 50 pence per month. Not bad, considering that I do not advertise!

-oOo-

A question I got was, "Why become a seeker, and what is the added value?"

In an earlier book, I posed that we are all seekers, either consciously or subconsciously. I hold to this belief. We may find people who do not want to know anything about spirituality, but they live a spiritual life when we study their behaviour. The reverse is also true.

I will attempt to answer the question.

We all follow a direction in life, either consciously or sub-consciously, which we feel is correct. How does one explain a feeling? We like football and become a fan of a team. We adore its players and follow every match. For some, becoming a seeker is like this experience. The issue with being a seeker is that what we seek is changing constantly. We learn, and we change. The added value may be the additional knowledge, but even this changes. Every living entity is a seeker; it is the conscious awareness that differentiates between those who admit and those that deny.

The path of the seeker is unique for every person. It starts with questions and eventually leads to realising that what we seek we can only find by following the inner path to becoming aware of the levels of consciousness we can access. As our capability increases, so does our awareness. What we seek and find today is different from what we seek and find tomorrow.

In this book, I touch on a lot of subjects which are feelings. Advanced seekers in this world tried to describe their experiences, and I tapped into this knowledge. Some of it I experienced myself. The path to discovering all aspects of our consciousness is, to me, beautiful. The learning is enjoyable, and the events we witness are great.

-o0o-

I once met somebody who told me that what we aim to achieve is not worth anything. Anyhow, what comes after completing the journey?

One answer would be that everything we do in life does not serve a purpose. We do many important things, and when we pass away, all that gets forgotten; it gets lost is the folds of time. Some actions of people linger on for some years; other deeds stay with us for centuries. Eventually, the memory of what we achieved disappears, but what last longest in the human race's shared memory appears to be some people's spiritual achievements.

Such an answer may well lead to extensive discussions with no beneficial outcome. In that sense, it is better to ignore the statement altogether.

People who say things like this are not yet ready to become a conscious seeker. We leave them where they are, at the material awareness level. They are happy; why disturb their happiness? Never try to explain to such people the why of a seeker. Such discussions lead to arguments, and a lot of anger may be the result. When a person is ready, they start seeking themselves, and when they come to us, we assist them. Be aware that a person who one day questions those on the path may come for help the next day. Always give in to a request for assistance; it is one of the tasks of a seeker.

-oOo-

I also got told that I am a Buddhist.

I do not mind somebody telling me such a thing, although I do not think the classification meant to be a compliment. I do not follow a religion, but I believe in certain aspects of how we should live this life. If my way of life and my writing means I appear to follow Buddhism, so be it.

My considerations about life and the meditation I follow are part of Sant Mat Yoga, a way of thinking that does not follow any religion. However, it uses Buddhist, Hindu, and Sikh thinking. Sant Mat also follows Sufi thought, and even the considerations of Christian thinking are found in Sant Mat. Of course, we can ask which of these philosophies came first, but is this question relevant? The reality is that people who follow the spiritual path, any spiritual path, should not, and usually do not, oppose each other. All seekers know that each person follows a unique path up to a certain level of awareness. After this point on our journey, we all follow the same direction. Judging which path is the only right direction to follow is not the way of the seeker.

When we arrive at the point where all path's combine into one, we may look back and realise our previous journey's futility. However, this is not how to think; when we climb a ladder, we may regard the steps below us as useless. Maybe they are now, but to get to where we are, these steps were essential. To love all living entities, we need to appreciate their journey and assist when asked and required,

Although my writing in this book may look as if I know the truth, it is not my intention to give this impression. Those that read my earlier books will detect quite a few changes and differences. Such is the reality of following the spiritual path. As life is subject to continuous change, so is all we encounter, including my thinking.

Enjoy this book, and any questions directed to me will be answered.

-o0o-

What this book intends to achieve

In my previous book, The Alternative, I deal with the process of meditation, but I linked the story to the art to develop the concentration of our attention. The ultimate aim of this is to explore the many levels of our consciousness. In this book, I intend to explore consciousness and look at what this concept means at the various spiritual levels. A lot of the information you, as a reader, will find in this book is a collection of information found in spiritual literature. However, I created myself the explanations of the meaning of the various terms and domains and their interpretations. Using words to explain anything that goes on in our consciousness, other than at the material awareness level, is nearly impossible. Therefore, we must expect that alternative ways of explaining the experiences are possible. There is no certainty about anything in the creation. Keep this in mind when digesting the way I describe it all.

-oOo-

At the material awareness level, most people assume that nothing else exists other than their present experience. The world is real; we can touch everything, and what else can there be? However, somehow, we feel that there is more. Our scientists tell us that whatever we feel is not real; it amounts to an illusion. We cannot measure feelings, and our senses are not equipped to comprehend these feelings. We do not know where they come from and why they happen. The result is that we often ignore our feelings and class, whatever we do not grasp, and what nobody can prove to exist, as "Nothing" or equivalent terms.

Our scientists try to measure feelings, but this relates to what we own and illnesses we do not have. What happens is that they look for their measurements to the outside world. As feelings are part of the inner path of our being, comprehension will not occur. Understanding that there are things that we cannot measure is something that we need to grasp.

It appears that the area covered by the term "Nothing", as discarded by ordinary people and our scientists, covers a lot of ground. When I read spiritual literature, the masters of the past and the present tell us about various concepts, which, when looked at with an open mind, appear to fill the gap nicely.

-o0o-

Scientists in psychiatry attempt to measure feelings, but they follow the rule that we must be objective. It is not easy to change a subjective reality like a feeling into an objective measurable entity. However, progress, based on studies and measurements, led scientists to conclude that psychiatric issues are often not with the patient; a change in society is the only way to change certain deficiencies.

When we attempt to measure feelings, we tend to work with duality; We recognise and define the concept of normal. Any deviation we regard as abnormal.

Another issue is that a person can subconsciously focus their attention on something specific from a very young age. Doing this can lead to what we call a psychiatric deficiency. We may call it a kind of addiction, which runs seriously out of hand. When people get into this mindset, they may hear voices and see ghosts. Such experiences are not spiritual; they relate to steering the mind in a single direction.

Treating any addition is very difficult, as it relates to a mindset. An addictive person tends to blame the outside world for what goes on in their life. When treating this deficiency, the person assisting often gets the blame for lack of progress, and treatment stops.

We can consciously focus our attention on a specific activity. By doing this, we move the spirit, spread over our body to a focal point in our head. When we focus properly, we push to other awareness levels, called the astral plane. As we do it consciously, we do not relate it to an addictive mindset. We work on our spirituality.

Although this may sound a bit esoteric, it happens all the time. When we put in a lot of effort to drive a car, we suddenly master the trick, and it becomes automated. The alchemists of the past knew this trick and tried to change lead into gold. Their real objective was to change their awareness level during their work from the average "lead" to a higher level of awareness, the "gold" level.

-o0o-

Most of humanity believes in a single higher entity we possibly call God, but other names exist depending on those who believe. In the past, people created religions based on a large number of such deities. Should we automatically discard the multiple God-like entities, or did the people who lived in the past knew something that we have not re-discovered up to now? Why do humans create a God-like entity at all? Why do we not live our lives in this world and accept that this is all there is? We often say that this world is our only reality, so we could live our lives following what we preach. By analysing personalities, I tried to provide a way of thinking that mixes modern scientific thought with the past and present spiritual reflections.

Meditation is a process that rapidly expands in modern society, and many variations are in existence. Each of these systems has its teachers, experts, and gurus. Psychiatric treatment includes some of these systems, learning to focus attention aims in such cases to solve issues.

For example, medical specialists often recommend mindfulness to solve typical stress issues in our society. We cannot solve every psychiatric problem with meditation techniques, a statement contested by masters of spirituality. This book is not about defining solutions to every possible psychiatric illness. However, we recognise that effective discipline of the way we use our mind will sort a lot of stress and focus related issues.

What happens in our modern society, people convert the concept of meditation into a business opportunity. It is an excellent way for some to earn a living by offering others the promise of a system that solves the stress issues created by modern-day living.

However, the original idea of meditation is different. In the East, there are still people who practise meditation the old-fashioned way. Those people use it to explore the layers of our consciousness, and they attempt to access these layers and create an awareness of the totality. They introduced their way of meditating to the West, and the number of followers keeps increasing.

It is essential to find out what those people try to achieve and deduct what we can find. When reading on, the reader will realise that I go further than only finding out what these people do; by analysing and executing meditation, I established that "Nothing" contains many realities that we did not yet discover with our scientific tools. It also became clear that the concept of "Nothing", or not-a-thing, should not exist in our vocabulary. There is always something, and our perception of not-a-thing means that we have not yet discovered what the "thing" is.

-o0o-

During the period that I developed my awareness to figure out what goes on, I also managed to create explanations of certain awareness levels, which I never found in the literature I studied. Of course, I did not read everything available, far from it. Others likely followed a similar path that I took to discover what we class as our consciousness. Many things mentioned in the chapter about consciousness came from those who managed to access these awareness domains. The analysis of their discoveries is mine, based on what I experience or what I expect to find.

What I purposely left out is the explanations about the material body and its chakras. There is lots of literature on the market about these subjects. We intend to explore the higher levels of our consciousness. Therefore, these chakras are not relevant to this book. We have 141 chakras, 7 of which are the main energy distribution points in our material body. Nice to know, but as we venture to explore the spiritual, we do not need to explore these in detail.

People often have spiritual experiences, and mostly, these are regarded as odd or as dreams. I believe that such events are part of the concept of "Nothing", and I tried to explain where these, in my view, originate. It is too easy to put everything we do not understand in a big bag with the label; "Nothing". When things happen, we need to openly discuss the matter and locate those we hope can come up with an explanation. We probably end up with many answers from people who regard this as an opportunity to earn money, but that happens anyway. Whatever people do and experience, there are always those that take advantage, with the sole intention to increase their earthly fortune. Whether increasing their wealth adds to their happiness and spiritual development is a different matter.

When studying spiritual concepts, I came across the audible lifestream. My present study direction is Sant Mat Yoga, and my description of the sound current follows this line of thought. A reference to the sound current we find in most spiritual directions of thinking in one form or another. As an engineer, I consider it logical that something like this exists; in my view, we should eventually detect it with sensitive instruments. We can detect the vibration in all matter; why should we not learn to measure this vibration source?

-o0o-

When I deal with the way an initiate behaves, I try to indicate that such a lifestyle is not only for those who consciously follow the spiritual path. To achieve the aim of being able to access all parts of our consciousness, we need to follow a lifestyle that is in line with our objective. Becoming a living entity that can access all awareness levels of consciousness is the ultimate aim. As you see, I already change my reference to consciousness as a single entity. It is not our consciousness; it is a single unit that permeates all living souls.

The question, "why do this?" is irrelevant to me. Through people's existence, they felt the need to explore the world they live in, and the question of "why?" never deterred those that explored the unknown areas of our world. The human mind is curious, and eventually, more people will follow the path of exploring consciousness, which brings us to knowing what and who we are.

I met those that told me that such explorations do not appear to show us what is next. In their view, people like me want to achieve merely eternal quiet. I found that acquiring knowledge is an endless game. In a previous book, I used the following drawing to make the explanation clear.

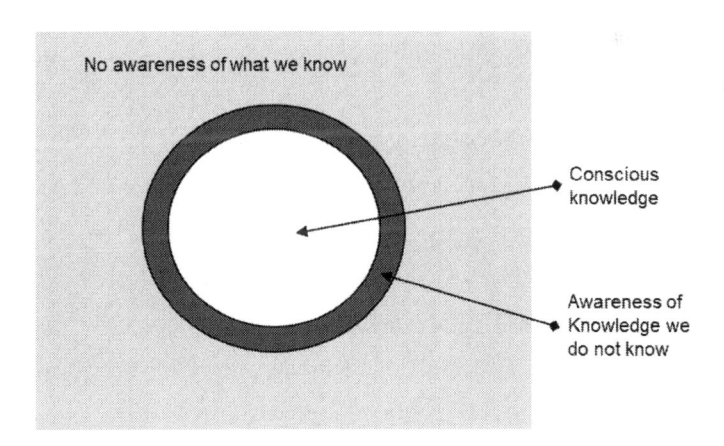

Our consciousness contains all knowledge ever created. We, therefore, can find whatever we need to know inside of us. However, as our focus is always on the outside, we perceive that we need to learn from others. The circles give an impression of the outside knowledge path.

At birth, our awareness of the outside world's knowledge is minimal; thus, the white, or inner circle, is small. We see, hear, and feel things around us, and we absorb this information. By doing this, we move items we are aware of to the white area. The circle becomes more extensive, and our knowledge increases.

The knowledge available at the material level of awareness is infinite. We will never be able to achieve a complete comprehension of everything. However, we found that we can achieve a higher level of understanding. Doing this allows us to have a grasp of everything at the lower levels. When people study a lot to become an expert, they achieve professional awareness and automatically a high understanding level. A professional engineer does this but consider a top sportsperson or an experienced painter of art. What such people achieve is to enter higher levels of their consciousness. Often, they can utilise this ability for related abilities as well.

Most people consider such an achievement normal; we call such humans experts in their field or, for sport, top sporters. Often, we declare that this skill is only for special people. When we avoid the acceptance of not being able to achieve this and analyse what goes on, we likely establish that such people learn to focus their attention to such a degree that they increase their awareness. Stress caused by major tournaments can cause this concentration of attention to decrease. The result is that what we can achieve during training cannot necessarily be matched during competition.

It takes a lot of repetition to train our attention to work under all conditions of stress.

-oOo-

In a way, we have answered the question, "why should we explore our consciousness?" People do this already, either in their professional work or as a sportsperson. We do it subconsciously because we are not aware of the spiritual action we take. All activities we execute during our life contain such spiritual content. Spirituality is not something for the few who want to become a monk and sit in isolation without speaking; it is a way of life that is part of what ordinary people do daily. What is different for those who do it formally is that there is a conscious awareness of what they want to achieve.

What I did in this paragraph is to refer again to our consciousness. The reality is that each of us perceives that we have a consciousness, which is ours. Compare it with a leaf on a tree. Each leaf assumes it is a single entity, but eventually, there is only one personality; the tree. All vegetation has roots that connect under the ground. Scientific studies indicate that, perhaps, all vegetation communicates, which is the basis for statements in the film Avatar. I deal with this effect in the chapter about personalities.

-oOo-

Spiritual literature indicates that the step from the physical to the spirit's domain of our consciousness is difficult; it requires the assistance of a person who achieved this feat already. We address this issue in some of the chapters. I agree that it is a step to no-mans-land, and therefore, people avoid this; why go to a place that nobody can tell us about or explain how we can comprehend what it means before we go? Those people will only go on holiday to a location if others can explain what they experience. Holidaymakers know this and create holiday brochures and video clips that show over-the-top explanations of how fantastic the area is. I tried to give an honest explanation, but in the end, I also made the experiences that we may face look excellent because they are. I did add the insecurities that we can experience, which are part of exploring areas that we never visited before.

-oOo-

The jump to what I call the nameless is another difficult feat, which I did not find in literature as being an issue. It is a step that requires us to forfeit the mind and the ego entirely. We go from an area that we at least partly understand to a phase that appears to be "Nothing"; we do not understand anything at all. The "Nothing" we now explore is real not-a-thing. However, this ocean of "Nothing" provides life to all entities that exist everywhere, provided that we accept that the term everywhere exists. The audible lifestream emanates from this "Nothing". As the nameless is everywhere, we will never be able to pinpoint the audible livestream's location. At all times, the sound current is where we are.

I believe in the concept of the requirement for initiation to start seriously on the path of spiritual development. However, as we find people in this world who, without any education, become better at specific skills than any teacher can be, I also realise that such people exist for the spiritual sciences. We can study what we want, but we may have to admit that we did not learn as much as we intended to learn at the material awareness level at the end of our lifetime. We also know stories about young people who achieved a lot without seemingly having to work for it. Life is like this, and we should never assume that others do not have to work. Each person follows their unique path in life. It is not our prerogative to judge whether somebody else is working or achieving. When we intend to accomplish a goal, our concentration should be on this goal, not on other followers' progress on the spiritual path.

The objective of the analysis in this book is to guide the reader along the path of discovering our consciousness, via the moment that we realise that "our" should not be used, to something we can only refer to as "Nothing". I do this with an engineering mindset, keeping the explanations relatively short.

To achieve this, I will explain my perception of consciousness, followed by elaborating on terms and expressions to improve an understanding of the subject. I added a chapter that details meditation to guide the reader on achieving awareness and a chapter on the astral level to show the reader that we can reach this level.

-o0o-

Consciousness

Describing a concept such as consciousness is not possible; it will inherently be simplistic. See it as a description of getting drunk. We may put a lot of effort in, but somehow, those who try it out see it differently, although most of them will agree that the next day is the worst day of their lives! Even the perception of the worst day of their life is for each person different.

Many feeling type concepts are like this; we can try, but eventually, we will not manage to give accurate descriptions. Butterflies in our stomach when we fall in love is another example. Some people may agree with the feeling until they realise that they never had butterflies in their stomach. They try to describe a feeling by comparing it with a feeling they never had. Of course, most people will now tell me that I am nit-picking, but we are seekers. The objective is to see the flaw in all we hear, even if we tell the story ourselves. Please read on, but keep this in mind.

-o0o-

Having made my point, I will try to give an impression of the various components of consciousness. The drawing below is an attempt to put together the experiences of those that explored consciousness. At the bottom end, we find, so it appears to us, our consciousness. However, after the areas we refer to as the physical, this idea of consciousness being ours slowly disappears. The mind does not rule past the physical, although its influence is still apparent for most higher regions. When explaining the drawing, I refer to personalities. Be aware that these are not like, what we at the material level of awareness refer to as persons.

Compare it with our body. When a cell in our body would manage to reach out to its higher entity, it will eventually meet the whole body, which we refer to as I. We are not aware of the cell in person, and the cell sees us as an ocean of cells, which combine in a single personality. However, we consider ourselves to be a complete and separate entity. All that follows below, we should treat by keeping this concept in mind.

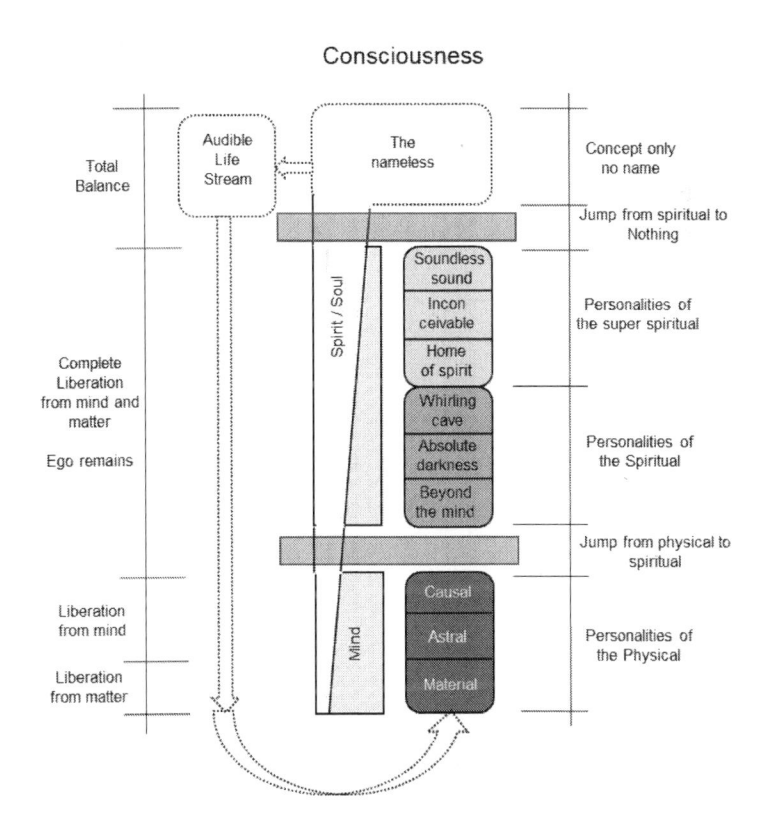

Consciousness

Total Balance	Audible Life Stream	The nameless	Concept only no name
			Jump from spiritual to Nothing
	Spirit / Soul	Soundless sound	
		Inconceivable	Personalities of the super spiritual
		Home of spirit	
Complete Liberation from mind and matter		Whirling cave	Personalities of the Spiritual
Ego remains		Absolute darkness	
		Beyond the mind	
			Jump from physical to spiritual
	Mind	Causal	
Liberation from mind		Astral	Personalities of the Physical
Liberation from matter		Material	

Ordinary people live entirely at the material level of their awareness. This is their world, they got born there, and they pass away in that world. For them, there is no other reality. This book describes something that cannot exist; what we explain here is equivalent to "Nothing" to ordinary people.

Every part of the material level of awareness is a living entity. Just like we regard ourselves as an entity, while in reality, we are the sum of 3,2 billion personalities, so is the material awareness level a personality, the sum of all those living at this level. Every character created is real, but it does not reflect what we, at the material level of awareness, regard as a person, i.e. it does not have a material body. However, it has everything else, like awareness and intelligence. Religions refer to the creator of the material awareness level as God. However, the real entity that encapsulates all that exists and created everything is much higher in our consciousness.

Some of us become aware of other levels of awareness in our consciousness. Somehow our body's senses appear separate. We achieve this via meditation and concentrating on the third eye. However, in cases of extreme stress, this can happen as well. The people who accomplish this become aware of the astral region. We can read a lot of stories about this awareness level. It usually gets described as very beautiful, and the lord of the Astral domain is majestic. The reality is different. Via the process of meditation, we can manage to feel the material body separated from the senses. A sign that this happens is that we become more aware of the world. We see things that we know we would not have noticed before. Life becomes richer and more colourful. Indeed, we can class this as impressive, but it appears as an everyday experience when it occurs. When we progress, we pull ourselves evermore into this richer world. In Eastern terms, "the Lord of the Astral Regions" is the entity that consists of all souls that manage to enter the astral level. The astral region is a lot larger than the material region, although we eventually find that time is an illusion. Based on this realisation, the concept of "large" also becomes an illusion.

Further progress with meditation guides us to the awareness of our consciousness's causal region, the mind's residence. This domain is vaster than the astral region. The mind controls these three physical areas of our consciousness, and it is the mind that created all our experiences by adding the dimension of time. When I say the mind, I refer to the single mind of the physical. All entities who reside in the physical have a mind, and these are part of the mind of the whole.

Time is a lot more important than we imagine. When we remove time as a factor, all other dimensions do not make sense anymore. What is left are personalities with feeling, awareness and intelligence. These are not next to each other; they are all one.

All physical awareness levels are attractive to us; the mind created this sense of beauty to copy the feeling we experience when we merge in the nameless. The objective is to tie the soul to the physical levels of existence.

The whole of the physical has a personality, which Eastern people allocated a name. This entity has what we refer to as the common mind, and it is the creator of all that exists at the physical awareness levels. Again, we may refer to this entity as God, as it is the creator of all that we can experience. Our task is to free us from the bonds that tie us to the physical, but this is difficult to do; we do not even realise what these bonds are, as these are part of our life, our culture. The sum of these bonds relates to the five vices, or, as I tend to call them, the five controls.

Anger and fear

Greed and desire
Attachment
Lust
Ego

Although the mind is entirely in charge at the physical awareness levels, the spirit or soul is also present, but in a minor way. The influence of the spirit increases when we manage to create a higher awareness of our consciousness. However, the mind has some effect at all times, which means that we can fall back to these vices from the material awareness level. These controls have a function: Only those that free themselves entirely from all the effects of these controls can enter the awareness level of the spirit, and eventually, the nameless. When we enter the awareness level of the spirit, we are still not loose from all the bonds that tie us to the physical; the mind can persuade us to return to the material level of awareness and fall prey to its desires.

The formal statement in spiritual writings is that we got tied with bonds or chains to the physical level of awareness. The reality is that these bonds relate to our desire to remain at these levels. We love the experience, even though we can prove it to be an illusion. There is nobody who ties us down. We do this ourselves by giving in to the five vices.

-o0o-

To create awareness of the higher levels of our consciousness, one path to follow is the process of initiation. We need to prepare ourselves by following a strict diet and learning to live by constant focusing on the third eye. These two requirements interact. When we eat meat, our concentration level diminishes, which hampers our meditation efforts. Such conditions are only effective in the early stages of spiritual development. When we connect permanently to higher awareness levels, we do not need such rules. However, those who reach these stages will adhere to the requirements.

Further, we need to clean ourselves from all effects of the five vices. This part of the process that leads up to initiation is exceedingly difficult. Initiation is regarded as the first serious step on the inner path, and as such, it constitutes the commencement of serious learning. Nobody expects the disciple to be perfect; he or she is at the start of a development program. Even at the higher levels, the possibility of giving in to the pleasures related to the five vices is still in existence. Proof of highly developed seekers who gave in to the material attractions is available for us to examine.

When we pass the initiation process and execute regular meditation, we learn to become aware of the audible lifestream. Initially, this will be a sound, very melodic and beautiful. The audible lifestream is the vibration of the creation; it is the force that created everything. When static energy meets the audible lifestream, the result is the creation of matter. At the higher levels of awareness, the audible lifestream is the force of positive creation, emanating from the nameless.

To move past the physical awareness level is a step from our ordinary level of experience to something that we never experienced. As this comprises a difficult step during our progress, the drawing shows an opening with a blue block.

When we enter our consciousness's spirit level, the mind's influence reduces, and the spirit takes over. The audible lifestream is still present, but we sense it differently. Some call it beautiful light; some refer to sound. At the highest level, there will be no sound. The reality is that the audible lifestream is part of the nameless, and it is everywhere. All that we experience, we only can sense because of this all-penetrating force. All our music can never be as beautiful as this unique vibration. When we first experience it, it changes our life forever.

The spiritual region, as a whole, also has a personality. Again, this is a real personality, although without what we refer to as a body. When we reach this level, we can meet the entity and even be in actual contact. Some people experience this, and their stories are that they met up with a fantastic person. This provides us with a description that attempts to compare an experience with something at the material level of consciousness. Effectively, such a person is a feeling that we experience, and it cannot fit into a description. However, just like we are real to us, so is this entity real to itself.

When we pass the domain of the spiritual, we enter the nameless. The environment of the nameless is where the audible lifestream originates. The audible lifestream flows down from the nameless as a single stream, creating all that exists. It then flows back up to the nameless domain in lots of different forms. How this all works is one of the mysteries of life.

We all feel that we are a personality, but we all consist of many single personalities. The higher we reach during our meditative feelings, the more personalities we encounter. Each of these personalities thinks that they are one. Eventually, there is only one out of all these innumerable personalities. Why is the creation like this; is there a purpose? We should remember that the concept of "a purpose" is something people invented, and it belongs at the material level of awareness. The creation does not necessarily have "a purpose".

There is no personality in the nameless domain, and naming it is not possible. A name at all times limits or frames something; as soon as we give it a name, it separates from all else. The nameless engulfs everything. Nothing in the creation and beyond gets excluded.

In the East, philosophers gave a name to this concept. Again, just like in the drawing, it suggests that this is an area we can reach. We do not have to go there; the nameless is everywhere. The art is to become consciously aware of something that is with us all the time.

One aspect of the nameless is that the mind lost its control completely. The concept of a personality relates to the ego; it means separation and duality. When something engulfs everything in existence, it can, by definition, not relate to duality and personality; it is everything.

The human being's design includes the mind and can only operate with dualities and the dimension of time. To even understand anything beyond these design features is beyond our capacity. We can climb up the ladder to other levels of our consciousness, but eventually, we need to climb down to create what we consider to be an understanding. However, we do this, and whatever we try, we never achieve complete comprehension of what life is all about. Such awareness is beyond human reach.

-o0o-

What sort of people achieve at least a basic comprehension of the concept of consciousness?

People who seek often have the impression that only Eastern monks spend sufficient time in meditation to get anywhere near to comprehending consciousness. Although some of these people manage to achieve reaching the nameless, it is not correct to assume that only those who contemplate many hours per day can achieve this feat.

We notice that people's perception leads to other persons dressing up in Eastern attire and showing their highly developed spiritual level via their knowledge and behaviour. To get their assistance, all we need to do is follow them to accumulate worldly assets, like money. When we wish to follow the path to spiritual mastery, avoid such people. They run a business at the material awareness level.

People who achieve a high level of spiritual awareness are precisely like ordinary people. We cannot detect any difference. Possibly we feel a solid attraction for such people, leading to a good friendship. When achieving such a friendship, we find that it leads to serious changes in our life. Do not expect such a person to be what we class as perfect; they are not. All we know is that our life is now different, richer, and more beautiful. Learn from such people, and follow them.

-oOo-

An analysis of the mind

To continue the story of how to follow the path, we need first to analyse the way we think and do what we do at the material awareness level.

I notice that people often confuse the brain and the mind. These two are different entities. In automation terms, the brain works like a PLC (Process Logic Controller), and it belongs entirely at the material awareness level. All information from our senses converts to electrical signals, and these transfer via our nervous system to the brain. The brain converts these signals to something the mind can comprehend. Everything we learn that the brain does, like producing pictures, holding our memory, etc., is, in reality, something that happens in the mind. The mind is not a material entity; it is the communication interface with our consciousness, and it creates the world we know.

When, due to illness, accident or age, the connection between the brain and the mind suffers, we assume that the brain does not function properly anymore. However, it is the interface between the two that does not work. Of course, we also recognise physical brain damage. Such an event causes communication between the brain and the mind to suffer, which, again, is an interface issue. Any situation that occurs related to our material body never influences the mind.

-oOo-

Now, what is the mind, and what does it do?

The mind is a very sophisticated and complicated tool, but it is a tool; it is not the entity that we call "I". In our civilisation, most of us humans consider that the mind is us, we call ourselves I am, and we mean the body and the mind. This belief is not correct; we have been given this body with a mind when we entered the material awareness level. However, the body belongs at the material awareness level, while the mind belongs only at the three primary physical levels of awareness. Our consciousness is where our soul resides and, as we learnt in the previous chapter, is an entity that covers all awareness levels.

The mind is not made out of matter, but it controls the physical levels of awareness. It also has some influence all the way to the spiritual levels of awareness. It is a tool that operates by comparing. We call this way of working duality. Due to this limitation, people will always think by comparing their experiences. Our programming allows no other way of thinking.

The mind is like a living entity, and it can start leading its own life. As an analogy, compare the mind with a very fancy sports car. If one is not entirely in control of the vehicle, the vehicle can take over, and the likely result will be a bad car crash. The car clearly can have a mind of its own. The mind is the same, it loves to be in charge of the body, and if we let this happen, we will lose all control; the mind becomes the body.

A master once told us that we could divide people into two main groups:

People that follow the mind.
People that follow the self - i.e. the inner master.

Those that follow the mind are, from my perspective, the majority of people. They believe that the world is real and the mind is equivalent to the brain and what they think they are. Seekers are people who know about the inner guide and the law of coincidence. Our soul is the inner guide, and it does not communicate in what we call at the material level of awareness a language. Language is the communication method of the material awareness level only. When we communicate with the soul, we receive messages in flashes when we use meditation methods, and we find our way in life by following coincidences.

Ordinary people do not believe in the law of coincidence. They love to use terms like luck and slight chance and various other ways to indicate their fortune or misfortune. These people believe that luck and chance are a part of their life. A seeker understands that coincidences happen in their life, and they follow these. Coincidences are one of the ways the soul communicates with us.

-oOo-

Our mind is a tool that likes to look back at previous experiences and make comparisons. We can observe this when we look at the concept of duality, which is how the mind operates. Everything in life at the physical awareness levels has two sides, and we compare them and judge which side we like the most. Memory is a collection of events based on duality. Unfortunately, duality only exists at the physical levels of awareness. The soul has no idea of the workings of this concept.

Give the mind something completely new, and it will not know what to do. It will create something that compares with previous knowledge so that it can develop understanding. As long as we assume that we are the mind, we will not think outside the box; the mind's design does not deviate from the norm. When we want to understand something completely new, we should do this without using the mind. Of course, this is not entirely possible as the mind is part of what we are, but we have to try. When we do this, we become a seeker; we will not follow the laws dictated by the mind; we follow our inner guide, originating from the spiritual awareness levels.

-o0o-

So, what is the real purpose of the mind?

So far, I see the mind as a gatekeeper. The mind created the physical world with its awareness levels, and we locked ourselves into this beautiful prison. The mind stands guard and will only let us progress to enter the spiritual awareness levels after learning all the lessons and have cleansed ourselves of all the feelings except the feelings of love and devotion.

This description comes from spiritual literature. These writings often explain that the mind is a separate entity; Sant Mat Yoga and various other schools of thought teach this way.

We can also assume that the mind is who we are, and we refuse to leave the physical world. We will only progress on our quest to explore the various higher levels of consciousness when all feelings that are not suited are under control. Only then do we start longing for the return to our real home, the spiritual awareness level. By thinking like this, we remove all the higher deities and angels of death from the equation. We are stopping progress; nobody stops us.

Our consciousness and the mind work together to achieve the experiences and development of the soul. The mind is the negative side of this duality, and the mind will always try to guide us to stay in the physical world. When we see the mind playing these so-called tricks, we should not regard these as bad; they are trials that the mind uses to test our resolve. We have to see this as part of the control system that we call our life. As long as we live in this physical world, the mind will keep on testing our resolve to move our attention to the spiritual level.

We call the mind the negative side of this duality as it tests our resolve by giving us material things that are an illusion. The mind is trying to push us back to the material world by offering material items we want but do not need. Every time we give in to an opportunity provided to us, it is a sign that our resolve is not yet sufficient. Our consciousness is the positive side of this duality. It tells us what we have to do to progress to the spiritual awareness levels. Our consciousness pushes us forward. However, both entities have one thing in common; they both have the same objective. Therefore, it is the art of the seeker to balance these two forces – see illustration below.

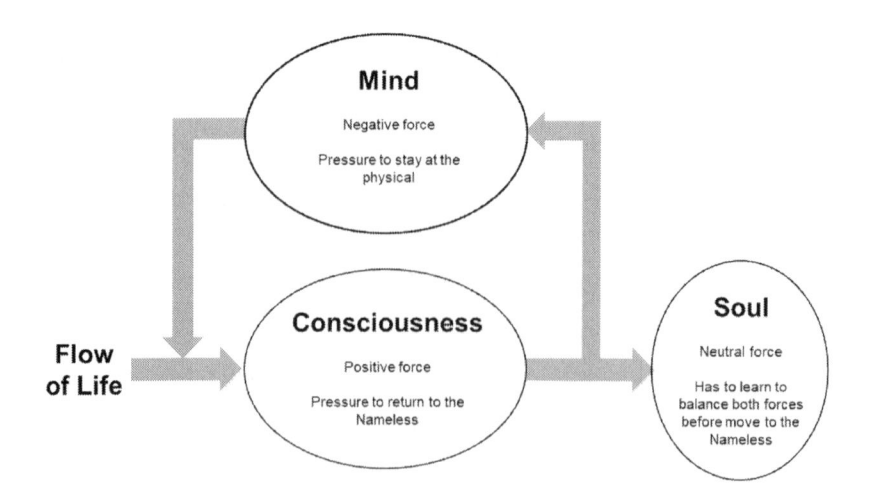

```
                    ┌─────────────────┐
                    │      Mind       │
                    │ Negative force  │
                    │ Pressure to stay│
                    │  at the physical│
                    └─────────────────┘
                      ↓             ↑
Flow          ┌─────────────────┐      ┌─────────────────┐
of Life  →    │  Consciousness  │  →   │      Soul       │
              │ Positive force  │      │ Neutral force   │
              │ Pressure to     │      │ Has to learn to │
              │ return to the   │      │ balance both    │
              │ Nameless        │      │ forces before   │
              │                 │      │ move to the     │
              │                 │      │ Nameless        │
              └─────────────────┘      └─────────────────┘
```

Note that our objective is to achieve a balance; we do not want to get rid of the mind; we want to balance the mind and consciousness. By achieving balance, and more control over the mind, we can move forward at a controlled pace.

All of nature operates like this; we find forward and reverse forces, which balance each other. Compare it with driving a car. The engine makes us move forward, but we avoid too high a speed by reducing throttle and the use of the brakes. We also use the steering wheel to adjust direction continuously. The combination makes us go towards our destination at a controllable speed.

Another observation is that the mind is not fighting against us, and it does not wage war with our consciousness of who owns the body. The mind wants to please us, and it does this in the best way it can. It tries to anticipate what we want, and it gives this to us in the only way it can. It copies our spiritual needs to the equivalent of what it can provide in the physical awareness levels. As it looks like the mind tries to divert us from getting back to where we belong – the spiritual and the nameless – it is assumed that the mind is trying to keep us at the physical awareness level.

Well, as the mind is part of this level, it has no conception of the existence of anything else, so why would the mind try to stop us? To the seeker, it may appear that the mind is fighting with us, but this is because we have problems with controlling its activities. When we can use the mind correctly, it can and will help us become aware of our consciousness's higher awareness levels.

The whole story appears to be about entities like the mind and our consciousness being separate and leading their own lives. This part of the story is not entirely correct. We are the only living entity; all these other entities are a part of us. When the masters of the past told us stories about the separation of consciousness into different entities, they did this to create understanding for their followers.

In the end, there is only one consciousness. We will have to learn this fact at some stage during our spiritual development, and by then, we will see the same issue as I now see; how to create an understanding for others who are listening. I am telling the story now as I see it because I firmly believe that the world is ready for another way of informing people about reality. However, the way I tell the story still needs testing. Are people willing to listen?

-o0o-

At birth, we received this tool called the mind, and because we do not control it as intended, the mind goes in a direction it thinks that it should go. When we learn to exercise control, the mind will follow us, and the fight is over. We got born into this material world as a separate entity. The mind follows this concept and creates something to separate us; we refer to this creation as our "ego". To a seeker, it appears that the conquest of the ego is the most challenging thing to do, and this is correct. We have to conquer the various controls used by the mind in this material world. When we learn to use all the commands used by the mind correctly, we are ready for the next step; to become aware of our consciousness's higher awareness levels.

Do not think that once we know how to use the mind, the fight for control is over. I keep referring back to the fancy sports car; once we become an excellent driver, we still have a good challenge on our hands to control the vehicle; it never becomes a piece of cake, so to say, but it will become much more manageable.

The past and present masters refer to a fight with the five evils, as people have always been at war; they understand the concept. When they would discuss the idea of five controls that we have to learn to use, there would not be any comprehension, and the objective was to create understanding. We trust that present-day seekers understand my explanation, as the world appears to be ready for this change in direction. It is so much easier to see everything as beautiful rather than seeing life as a constant fight!

-o0o-

Due to humanity not being in control of the mind, we are on the road to possible self-destruction. The mind rules humanity instead of humanity governing the mind. We received a priceless gift when entering the material level of awareness; now, we must learn to get this gift under control before the gift destroys us. We cannot blame the mind for this; nobody should blame their tools – well, I have personally blamed my saw for not getting in a straight line through a piece of chip wood, so I have to be careful with this statement! The issue is that some of us know what is required, but how do we convince the majority of the people to follow this path?

The answer to this question is that we do not try to convince others. Convincing others can lead to controlling others and looking down on those that do not follow the right direction, our direction. When we do this, we will be back in the material world, playing our role in the theatre of life.

We do what requires doing in our unique way. By doing this, we will be an example for others, and we look at others with love and not with disdain. Never forget that we have been there ourselves, and we did not like it when people looked at us as if we were not reacting correctly. Good example without disdain for others creates followers. We would like to create those that follow, but we do not want to create a cult type organisation with followers that hate the rest of the world or even look down on the rest of the world. Again, we see the balancing requirement.

-o0o-

The mind receives a lot of incoherent information from our body sensors, and it needs to understand what is going on in a material world type of understanding. Therefore, the mind created the dimension of time, and via this creation, brought the material world to life. By introducing time and reduced sensitivity of our senses, the mind made the physical awareness levels in a beautiful and attractive filmlike illusion that gives us fantastic experiences. However, we have to get to the comprehension that all this is the power of creation of the mind. The actual creation is a projection by the mind on our consciousness, and it is nowhere else. What goes on is beyond our understanding.

The mind is a physical world entity, and it has, therefore, severe limitations. When we follow the spiritual path, there will come a time that the seeker will want to go beyond the physical awareness levels and to achieve this, the seeker will have to shed the use of the mind. The mind – up to that moment – has been a fantastic tool, but when we go beyond the causal level of awareness, we no longer require the mind's use to continue the progress on the spiritual path. When this moment comes, the mind will start to become a liability. Be aware of this and love the mind for how it has shown us the way in a negative way but be prepared to shed the mind when the time comes.

When we go beyond the casual awareness level, we will still be aware of being ourselves. The reason for this is the ego part of the mind; we believe that we are a separate entity. Masters, therefore, say that to shed the ego is the most challenging thing to do; we have to realise that we are not a separate entity; we are one. Initially, being one will be that humanity becomes a single independent entity, but eventually, there is only one in the whole universe, and we are part of this one.

-o0o-

A specific issue of the ego is that we are constantly feeling threatened and essential. A lot of what we do is to impress others, and this activity is feeding our ego. When we become very famous, the attention we get will inflate our ego. Unfortunately, this does not only lead to wanting more and more attention. In many cases, it also leads to looking down on others, making others feel irrelevant. This behaviour causes these others to fight even harder to prove themselves. We have now identified an issue in the material world that leads to constant war. Be not mistaken; we fought quite a few real battles purely to satisfy some powerful people's ego.

The feeling to want to be meaningful and the wish to be recognised is what drives people to achieve, and as the material world requires people who perform, we should not discourage this feeling. However, it is something that seekers should not encourage in themselves as we need to conquer our ego, not cause inflation. Many of the masters tell us that the further we develop on the spiritual path, the more we become servants of humanity. This statement's objective is to emphasise the need to suppress the feeling of being separate; we should conquer the ego and become part of the whole. We should concentrate on being a servant and train ourselves to love everything alive.

This chapter mentions many times people and their reactions based on the workings of the mind. We will deal with the concept of personalities to bring more structure to the path that we describe as "Nothing".

-o0o-

Personalities

We dealt with the mind's concept. So, what constitutes a personality, and why is this important to know for a seeker? In this chapter, we show that all that is in existence consists in some way out of structures created by the mind; we call these personalities. The reason for this way of thinking is that the creation is up to the highest spiritual level, an illusion, with the mind's involvement at every level, causing the ego to produce personalities. We do not comprehend anything else; the reality, to us, is immaterial.

-o0o-

How do I define a personality?

A personality consists of a group of entities with some form of commonality. Such a group can be tiny; even a single person creates personalities, depending on the environment.

Human beings start their existence at the material level of awareness. When merged at this level of awareness, we tend to assume that we are a single entity, and with this comes our personality. However, each human consists of around 3.2 trillion cells, each with a personality. Cells have an average lifetime of about seven years. Depending on where the body uses cells, their lifetime varies considerably. It differs from a few days in the skin to an identical lifetime as the human body in parts of our brain.

The body has components called organs and a skeleton. Each of these parts is a combination of lots of cells and has a personality. The heart pumps blood around the body to supply all the body parts with their needs, while the brain controls the elements based on the mind's instructions.

The sum of all these different components working together as a team makes the human body function as a single unit. We call the awareness that exists in this unit our personality.

Now let us go a bit further.

Some ordinary people analyse how a person looks, and this shows them – in their view – their personality. Other people take this concept and change the way they look via makeup, Botox, and medical changes to their bodies. These changes create the body they desire; it goes with what they perceive to be their personality. Many ordinary people take the example of the few, copy what these people do, as they love to have an identical look, and, hopefully, they get a similar personality.

We examine other people, and when we like what we see, we attempt to copy them.

Fashion relates to this way of thinking, but the wish to attract many others' attention and become famous also is one of the considerations. The words we use and how we phrase them get all adjusted to what we perceive others like to hear from us. We create a personality based on what we hope attracts others. We eventually create a cheap caricature of who we are; we lose our original personality completely; it hides behind all the changes we made during the initial period of our life.

Each of the changes constitutes what I call a little role play on the stage of life. Khalil Gibran calls it that we wear a lot of masks in his short story, The Madman. Spiritual literature often refers to the chains that tie the soul to the physical awareness levels. All these statements are in their way correct; they indicate how we dedicate our lives to living at the material awareness level. We look outward; we do not follow the inner path.

What we do not realise is that each of us is unique. We consist of lots of separate personalities, and the sum of all these individual parts is our personality.

An example of this system is that we can mix well with a friend, but when he is together with a few others, we think he changed; he is not the person we know. We see that our friend is now part of a group, he identified with the assembly, and this group created a separate personality.

Expert crowd managers understand that they need to address the group when they stand in front of a crowd. At that moment, the sum of the people has its personality; to manage the group requires a different approach from working its components.

A well-known comedian told a reporter that he imagines himself standing in the crowd when he addresses the audience. When he looks at himself at the stage, it shows him how people perceive him. His statement indicated that he knew how to manage a crowd. Being both inside the audience and on the stage, he created a new entity by emerging himself inside the group.

-o0o-

Creating such entities keeps on going until we find the all-encompassing personality we are presently aware of; the creator of us all, mother earth. We can keep on observing created groups in the region of consciousness that contains detectable items. Eventually, we arrive at the personality that engulfs the whole of the creation, the creator of the universe. We may, in our innocence, assume that the universe does not have a personality. However, it has, and it is an entity with awareness and intelligence. Eastern spiritual masters created a name for this personality, and they tell us that we can become aware of this entity via proper meditation.

Such a meeting is difficult to describe. We do not encounter a person; we are in touch with an entity that combines awareness and intelligence. To compare the experience with our body: We do not have an awareness of the individual components in our body; when these cells manage to become aware of us, they merge consciously into our awareness. Meeting the creator of the universe will be a similar experience. We become aware of him; he is not aware of us.

We now come to the essence of the workings of a personality.

A personality consists of a group of components, which changes when some of its members change.

We may think that we are still the same personality we were when we got born, but we are not. The mind uses our memory and our ego to create the impression that nothing has changed, and we are still the person we were when we got born. However, after a few years, we are different.

Every time cells die, the body replaces them with new cells, resulting in a change in our body's personality. Such changes are minor, but they are changes.

-oOo-

Each personality has some form of intelligence, awareness, and consciousness. As the components change when time goes by, the parts change; thus, the totality changes.

Everything that we consider as our reality is constantly changing.

Humans love their lives to be steady. We try to create something we refer to as stability, but this is impossible. The whole structure and design of the universe constantly changes its components and, thereby, its personality. Most parts live a lot longer than a human being, which feeds our belief that a form of stability is achievable. When we study the universe's workings, it soon becomes clear that such an assumption is an illusion.

When we look at history, we have difficulty establishing what happened around 1000 years ago. Humans of that period likely felt that what went on was highly important; like we now think that what happens in our world is essential. In the way the universe operates, what we do individually is of little concern. This fact is a lesson that humanity does not yet fully grasps. We are of little concern when seen in the overall creation.

Each component of the universe has a limited lifetime, and when such an item passes away, some other piece takes its place.

When we study the universe, it appears logical that eventually, all its components will disappear into what we term as black holes. These black holes swallow each other, and we end up with a single black hole that contains everything that we define as matter. Possibly this single black hole is not stable, it explodes, and a new universe gets born. Signs that this process has happened before are there, found by our scientists.

When such an event happens, likely, all personalities disappear, and after the explosion, new personalities develop over time. The story of the development and retreat of the universe looks like everything else in life; it constitutes a process of constant change, dying, and rebirth.

-oOo-

Real meditation aims to focus our attention on becoming aware of the regions within our consciousness related to the spirit levels. We do this by concentrating our attention on the third eye. After practice, we reach an awareness level not governed by the mind and without the dimension of time. What this entails we cannot comprehend, but we can understand that a body as we know it does not appear logical.

Speaking requires the use of language and the vocal capabilities of our material body. Also, a language requires the dimension of time; thus, communication will be vastly different. Those who managed to concentrate their awareness on this region of consciousness tell us about meeting a personality, the lord of the spiritual world. Based on logical considerations, it cannot be possible that they met a physical person. It is conceivable that they met a personality, an entity with awareness and intelligence. By using the limited capabilities of the mind, their experience got translated into meeting a person.

We clarified some of this explanation in the drawing below:

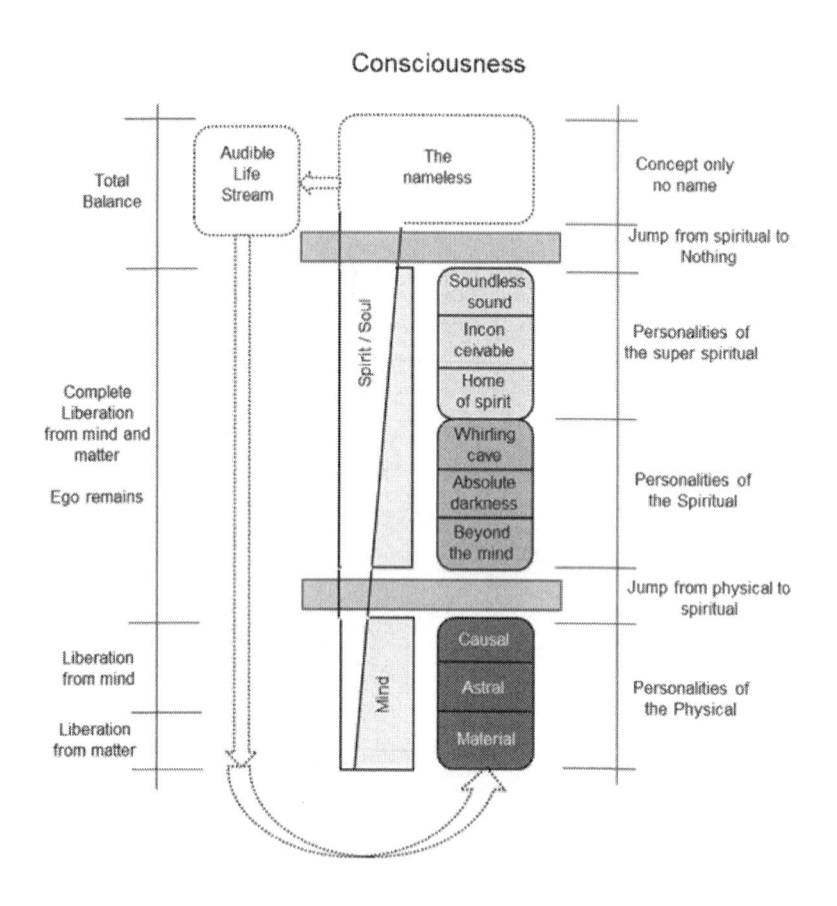

Consciousness

Left labels	Center	Right labels
Total Balance	Audible Life Stream / The nameless	Concept only no name
		Jump from spiritual to Nothing
Complete Liberation from mind and matter	Spirit / Soul: Soundless sound, Inconceivable, Home of spirit	Personalities of the super spiritual
Ego remains	Whirling cave, Absolute darkness, Beyond the mind	Personalities of the Spiritual
		Jump from physical to spiritual
Liberation from mind	Mind: Causal, Astral	Personalities of the Physical
Liberation from matter	Material	

When exploring our consciousness all the way up, we discover numerous personalities. These are not persons as we know them; however, they have intelligence and awareness. These personalities do not necessarily have a material or physical body. When we become aware of these entities, in effect, we merge in their awareness; we become part of the personality.

The process of initiation allows us somehow to experience these personalities as physical persons. However, it is not proper to assume that they are separate persons because they are not. They are the summary of their component parts, and we are one of these components.

As long as we can experience separate personalities, we are still under the influence of the mind, although this influence is retreating the higher we focus our attention.

The explanation shows that there are many personalities, which are a sum of numerous personalities like us. We could refer to these as Gods. Eventually, there is a single highest level personality. We established a ranking system with multiple God-like entities and one overall leader. Rather than discussing lots of Gods, it seems better to refer to personalities.

-o0o-

In Eastern belief systems, all the areas of our consciousness that are considered separate have a God or Lord in charge of that domain.

We conclude that wherever we find a personality, we still experience influence by the mind, as creating a personality involves the ego.

When the ego is finally gone, we do not find any more personalities; we moved our awareness to the nameless. The drawing shows the nameless, but this is a simplistic drawing. Showing the nameless is not possible; the nameless is all that exists. Whatever we see or touch, whatever we know is there, it is part of this entity. From the analysis, it seems incorrect to dismiss the concept of numerous Gods and replace these with the One.

All assumptions are correct; there are many creators, but eventually, there is just One.

The nameless is in perfect balance. Due to this, it comes over to observers as "Nothing". With our senses, even when extended with sensing tools, we can only detect things that are not in balance. As soon as the vibrating energy is in perfect harmony, the vibration ceases to exit.

-oOo-

When the mind loses its dominance and the spirit takes over, we enter the spirit area. This domain has a personality, but it is permanent in its existence. When the big bang at the physical level occurs, this part of consciousness is not affected. However, it does change regularly; new components keep on entering and leaving.

Permanence in our consciousness is not a concept that exists. Permanence is a dream of people; it is not part of reality.

I, purposely, talk about personalities. Although we would like to see these entities as persons having a human form, this is not the reality. We can communicate with these personalities when we reach the proper awareness level. However, bodies are not part of what we experience, and communication does not involve a language.

Any communication with a higher entity is from high to low. Being aware of an entity is from low to high.

As humans, we can comprehend what a higher personality thinks, we can apprehend its awareness and intelligence, and we can feel its personality. It is not likely that we can have a conversation.

-o0o-

The forgoing on the creation and manipulation of personalities leads to a far-reaching conclusion:

By focusing our attention to reach an awareness of the totality of consciousness, we align all lower-level personalities.

When we, via the process of meditation, focus our attention on the third eye centre, intending to reach an awareness of the higher levels of consciousness, we will, as a side effect, align all lower-level personalities of our existence.

Although I now appear to discuss a human being, the alignment applies to all personalities. Those who enter the spiritual level have aligned themselves sufficiently to reach, at the material level of existence, an alignment that avoids creating new karma, i.e. an unbalance of the energy levels.

When we go through initiation, we receive some portion of such a personality from the person who does the initiation. As an initiate, we need to nurture this portion, and when our whole body permeates this, we automatically lose all residual karma.

Even a person who works hard to focus their attention on aligning their thoughts and actions with the objective to follow their inner guide will eventually lose all deviations and move to the spiritual levels of consciousness.

The process of alignment always works. Initiation is one way, but other paths exist.

An obvious question now is: How to become ready?

We deal with this in the next chapter.

-o0o-

Preparation for the Path

Getting prepared for the move to gain awareness of the spiritual involves a lot of work. It is not an easy task; we need dedication and perseverance. A lot of the information I put in this chapter I derived from "The Path of the Masters" by Julian Johnson. However, it is common Eastern knowledge.

I found as well that the preparation for a masonic master degree contains a lot of similar requirements. In Eastern terms, we need to achieve Vivek. Below I attempted to describe what this term entails.

The mind contains four phases, which we describe as follows:

Scattering. A human tends to have thoughts going all the time in various directions, which are often repetitive. It isn't easy to control this habit. Science found that when we change our behaviour for about four weeks, we create another behaviour pattern. By commencing this phase, we force ourselves to think thoughts that we know are relevant and useful. After four weeks, we developed a habit, and the task of avoiding scattering becomes easier. Be aware that the practice of constant thinking never goes away; it is simple to get stressed, and a lot of repetitive thoughts fill up our day-to-day thinking pattern again. Compare it with stopping other habits, like smoking. When we stop, it becomes more comfortable after a few weeks, but the craving does not go away.

Darkening. A lot of our thoughts can escalate into dark thinking, laziness and evil. It is inherent in human nature to try to avoid strenuous activity. When we must execute such work, we blame others because we have to perform such a difficult task for a prolonged period. When we start controlling our mind, we notice that it is easy to have uncontrolled flawed thinking about whatever goes on in our existence. Such thoughts lead to a change in behaviour and can even lead to action. We need to avoid converting evil thoughts into doing something, but eventually, we need to avoid having these thoughts at all. The best way to prevent darkening is to take full responsibility for all that goes on in our life. When we take this action, the blaming and judging of others will reduce, and our mind clears up.

Gathering. This term relates to the controlling of scattering and darkness. In this step, we start control of the first two mental phases. It is the preamble to concentration. Although we define this phase as a separate mental step, it relates to the fourth step. We are not yet ready to completely control the mind, but we, at least, are consciously aware of the issue and attempt to avoid the activities of the mind which we consider useless. A lot of the meditation exercises in the Western world relate to this phase. It involves the discipline of the mind to avoid the stress which goes with our lifestyle.

Concentration. When we get the first three phases under control, we are ready to start learning the art of concentration. We can now learn to focus our attention on the third eye. This part allows us to commence real meditation, which we require to follow the path to awareness of consciousness's spiritual level. I dedicated the last chapter of this book to real meditation, which I also call the art of reaching awareness of our consciousness's higher levels.

-o0o-

After describing what the concept of Vivek entails, we need to go into the various steps that prepare us for becoming aware of the totality of consciousness. Of course, being of Western mindset, the question may come up: "Why go through all this hassle? Can we not just go there?" The answer is that when we do not prepare, we do not want to go there. We do not get stopped by anybody else; we do not wish to proceed on the path.

We need to develop a flawless morality.

The life we lead must be one of caring, giving to those in need and in general, being classed as good. Over-indulgence is not the way; giving in to our desires, lust, and greed must stop. We have five vices; anger, greed, attachment, lust and ego. The flawless mentality refers to conquering the first four.

Never forget that these rules got written down in 1939. These days people accept that following the path starts by learning, not by being thoroughly prepared. However, the expectation is that we at least try. See it as a symbolic requirement. We try, and at times, we fail. When we have the correct attitude, we keep on trying. Doing this is sufficient to classify the behaviour as flawless morality. Perfection comes after a lot of work; we do not create it by concentrating and saying, "I want to be perfect!"

We need to emphasise that nobody will stop a person who wants to follow the spiritual path. When we do not wish to follow the rules, we just stop ourselves. We can visit the sat sang of a master regularly, and on the outside show that we are ready. Being prepared as a mindset is not identical. As long as our feelings still convey the vices' signs, we cannot claim to be ready, and we will not move to the level of the spirit.

We stop ourselves; there is nobody else to blame for our lack of progress.

We need to lead a well-organised life.

We lead an organised life, and everything we do steers us from getting ready for following the inner path. It is essential to get familiar with spirituality, so reading and listing to the sat sangs of a master is critical. We should carefully examine all our actions; are they useful? It is amazing when doing this to find that most of our activities are not helpful. We get back to the scattering described above. We do not just think repetitively; our actions come from habitual behaviour, which is often not very useful when looked at from up close. Organisation means to be consciously aware of what we do, analyse our activities, and ensure that we only execute practical activities.

Especially in our Western culture, we do a lot based on speed. We rush through a supermarket, pushing others aside, and when we have what we need, we arrive at the till and try to move in front of others. We rush through the traffic, and when we come home, we do not know what to do next, other than watch the news on the TV. Was it indispensable to behave as we did? Could we, possibly, behave courteously to others? It may mean that we arrive home five minutes later. So what?

Lead a life of devotion and service.

We may sound like selling a religion, but that is not the meaning of the phrase. As a seeker and follower of the spiritual path, we assist all other people. We are not selective; when a person needs assistance and asks for assistance, we help.

We understand that we, in the end, are all one, so we learn to see the good in all life. There is good in everything we see, even if ordinary people consider the actions we observe as bad.

By turning our way of thinking around to such a way of living, we also add a loving component to the personalities we are part of; we change those for the better. The objective of a seeker is to bring about change for the better, and the way we go about this is to be ourselves better. We do not try to tell others to improve their behaviour.

We know that all life, wherever it lives, is part of One Life. Only by living this realisation can we learn to love everything that exists, however brutal its behaviour may be. When we learn to change our lifestyle like this, we start radiating love. We have surplus energy, and we give this subconsciously to all those that we meet.

Attain the correct mental attitude.

After reaching the phase that we can behave like the former descriptions, we now arrive at the part that we must learn to become this person. Nobody should tell us to live such a life; we are the reality and live like this automatically.

In this world, many people live a good life because it is expected of them by others. The seeker on the spiritual path must not follow the rule; they are the rule and the example.

At some stage during my life, I found a person who asked me the following questions:

> Do you want to be yourself?
> Do you want to behave like what others expect from you?
> Do you want to become what others expect from you?

These questions relate to the development of the human on earth. When we get born, we are ourselves. Due to pressures from the outside, we start behaving like we think that others expect us to act. Eventually, all these little theatre plays become what we are; the actual entity we are hides behind these compilations of masks.

To attain the correct mental attitude, we need to realise what our games are. We do not need to shed all our plays; we need to be consciously aware of what we do and who we are. By realising this, we can become the audience who watches the games we play and other people's games. We do not involve ourselves in the spectacle we call living.

Achieve mental detachment from the world.

We now arrive at the phase that we must take our distance from the living world and all affairs that go on around us. We do not become a hermit; we live an ordinary everyday life, we love our lives, and we love those that are part of our lives. However, we live it mainly as an audience. We detach ourselves from what happens. Do not underestimate the factor of detachment. When we think we achieve it, we already attach ourselves to the achievement. Absolute detachment means to live life without being involved; we are always at a distance, we view what goes on, but it is not part of what we are.

Work on the destruction of all desires.

Removal of our desires is the most challenging task to achieve. Even the thought of wanting to remove desires is a desire. We can only accomplish this feat by living all the other parts written down above. It is impossible not to have desires when we still have any greed, lust, and attachment working in our body. All these factors need to be under control before we can even begin working on our desires.

When the control of all these factors is part of our lives, we will be ready to pass the step to the spiritual. Do not assume that this is the final hurdle. We can fall back at any moment. We may think we are ready, and a beautiful looking car passes by. It takes a simple thought of desire to wipe out a lot of progress, and we need to start at the beginning.

There is only one way to kill the desire for low-level material items, which is to replace them with a higher level of desire. We follow and love our master. We wish always to be close to this person. The master knows this and creates this desire by taking measured distance from us. He shows us how to listen to the audible lifestream. When we achieve hearing the sound current, we can listen to this fantastic music and follow our inner guide. We now have the desire to be with the audible lifestream and the inner guide forever. Although it is still a desire, it helps us become aware of our consciousness's higher regions. Later on, we need to shed these desires as well.

-o0o-

Concluding the last two chapters:

A personality is a combination of awareness and intelligence. It does not necessarily have to be consciously aware of its existence, and it does not necessarily need a relationship with a material body.

Everything in existence is part of a personality. We do not recognise anything that is not part of a personality, except the nameless.

To follow the path to the spiritual level, we need to prepare ourselves. The reason for this is not that some high-level foreign entity stops us if we do not go through the process of preparation; we stop ourselves, as we do not wish to progress.

We require dealing with some other material awareness level issues before we proceed exploring the path to "Nothing". These are the concept of karma and our communication system.

-o0o-

The Concept of Karma

Most of us know about the subject of karma, and I wrote about it in previous books. To most, karma is the instrument that hands out punishment. We do something that is not to the liking of our God, and it converts into karma, which follows us all our lives and even in our next life.

My task is to put a more technical perspective on this concept. In this chapter, I attempt to give a different perspective on the subject linked to present-day science.

All through our lives, we take forms of action. One of the laws of nature is:

Action = Reaction

Whatever we do, and whatever we think, has an implication. It causes a reaction. All our thinking and our actions relate to the five vices, or, as I call them, the five controls exercised by the mind. The most vigorous control that relates to karma is our desire or greed. When we take any form of action based on something we desire, we cause a feeling. We know this feeling; it causes us to want to obtain the subject of our desire. Greed relates to desire; it is the feeling that drives us to get everything we desire. Attachment relates as well; it is the feeling that makes us hang on to the subjects of desire. We now identified a whole range of feelings, and these relate to actions. When we take action on our desires, we make feelings stronger, but even thinking about desires is an action, which causes a reaction.

The identified feelings related to greed and desire are energy in some form. We can create positive or negative forms of energy. To progress in achieving our mission to become aware of all aspects of our consciousness, we must somehow balance these energies and neutralise them to zero. No surplus energy should be detectable; we should have no remaining feelings. When we achieve this, our awareness reflects "Nothing". We can only travel on the path of the sound current when we neutralise the collected energy levels.

Translated into karma: We must pay off karma before proceeding on the path. Although this is the statement we find in spiritual literature, there is doubt. The mind is active to some extend at the spiritual awareness level; thus, we create karma. All through the journey towards our mission to become aware of the totality of our consciousness, we are experiencing aspects of the mind and the five vices.

We can hear the audible lifestream after we achieve to activate our inner ear, but there is still a lot of work to do on the way towards the highest region of our consciousness. The task we have is to balance energy on the way by taking the correct action. We do not become perfect, and after that, follow the path; we follow the path to become perfect.

Again I use the word perfect. To remind the reader, a perfect person means that they reached a total awareness of their consciousness. We are whole. We do not live in the dark anymore; we know who we are. Some describe this in initiation ceremonies as; to die and get born again. However, it cannot be a single step based on following a simple procedure; it is a development process that can take years.

-o0o-

During our life, we collect a whole range of deeds and wishes, which are in large part responsible for the way we live, and the creation of our personality. What happens to us relates to our personality; we, ourselves, cause all the events that go on in our lives.

This statement leads to challenges. "How can weather disasters relate to the way I took action in the past?" To answer this question and others of similar meaning, we go back to personalities. When a higher level personality takes action, such an event results in a reaction, just like the actions we take at our level. The body of our mother earth is such a personality, and her actions lead to reactions.

At our level of awareness, we do not know how mother earth thinks or takes action; thus, our understanding of events on earth and why they happen is minimal. However, there is always a relation between action and reaction; we cannot deny this law of nature. All through the universe, personalities take actions, and each of these actions results in a response. Why perfectly honest people may get hurt by a meteor falling towards the earth is one of these reactions.

To make this conclusion clear with an example at our level of awareness: When we have cancer, our oncologist may decide to remove the tumour. To do this properly, he needs to remove a lot of the surrounding healthy tissue. This explanation applies everywhere. Some actions touch perfectly healthy personalities. However, the action is required to avoid events running out of control.

When we pass away, our material body stays behind, and eventually, due to lack of awareness, it converts to dust. Our astral body, loaded with the collected feelings, leaves our body, and when the amount of feelings is excessive, we look for a way to satisfy our desires. The result of this process is that we enter the material world again in a new body.

The basis for the choice of the life we intend to lead is the collected feelings. The place of birth and the type of body relates to the actions we took in our previous life. In other words, we chose everything that happens to us before our birth. The choosing is not necessarily a fully conscious reaction; just like acquiring assets does not always mean that we know what we do; we give in to our desires.

When we use the way of thinking I proposed, we can explain many of the events happening in our lives, and we can explain why we enter life the way we do.

We need to be careful with the interpretation of the preceding. People tend to look at somebody and interpret what they see as punishment or reward. Doing this relates to the material level of consciousness, while the execution of all decision making happened at the highest physical level. We may decide that a rich person got rewarded, but this may not be correct. Such a person may need to learn a lesson – based on feelings experienced – how to deal with money. A poor person did not receive punishment; it may be a reward with a learning to let go of attachment. As we do not know what goes on at our awareness level, we should avoid judging anybody. We follow our unique spiritual path and let others go where they have to go. Judging is the worst action we can take when following spiritual considerations. Unfortunately, most people live by judging others, and those following the spiritual path are no different.

During our life at the material level of awareness, we are so occupied with the process of executing our desires and giving in to our greed and attachment that we will not take the time to listen to the audible lifestream. We do not need a lot of training and special treatment to hear this sound; we just do not take the time. People so often tell each other that they are too busy to meditate or contemplate life. However, they sit for hours in front of a TV, listening to news about places in the world they do not know. The conclusion is that making time is a matter of setting priorities. Nobody is too busy to look after their spiritual development.

-oOo-

How do we get rid of collected karma?

The issue is that we make around 60,000 decisions daily, and each of these causes a reaction. Both the action and response lead to the collection of karma. Over a lifetime, we generate a lot of this energy unbalance, and to sort this out is nearly impossible. However, nature always provides ways to allow progress in life, and in this case, we can progress by following the messages of our inner master. The process appears simple, but when we try it out, it is not easy at all.

Whatever happens to us, accept it, as it is something that we must endure.

> Be happy with challenges; they buy off karma.

Be happy when some person insults us; they take away our karma.

Do not indulge when good things happen to us; we give in to attachment.

View life from a distance, as an audience. Do not get involved.

See life as a fantastic experience, but do not get attached.

We can work on these instructions for a long time, and suddenly something occurs that sets us back. Even thinking about how to treat somebody who broke into our house creates karma. The short recommendation is to go with the flow of life. Do not resist or try to change what goes on; live life as it comes to us.

What we find is that at all times, it is the desire that causes us to fail. It is so easy for us to like something and attempt to obtain the item. Only when we challenge it we realise that we can appreciate something without owning it; we can admire sceneries without buying the land. We can enjoy fish in the sea without purchasing an aquarium and filling it with fish.

It is the obtaining action that gives us, temporarily, a good feeling. As soon as the item is in our possession, we look for other things to satisfy our feeling. Conquering this feeling is very difficult. The best advice is to challenge everything we intend to obtain; for ourselves and others. Make sure that we really need the item. We may find that, eventually, we need very few things.

I questioned many people by looking at the difference between must-have and would-like-to have during my working life. We need to take such action for what we intend to obtain.

Do we need to live like a hermit?

We are in the world to live our life. Doing things that are not natural to us will not assist in our development. It is possible to live an ordinary life, marry, have children, go out with friends, and at the same time create a form of detachment from all our experiences. It will be a constant process, but it is rewarding to know that whatever happens will not affect us, as we are the audience; we are not playing a role in the theatre of life.

When we live like this, our collected karma will reduce. However, there is collected karma from previous lives. To sort this out, we require assistance from a master. During the initiation process, this person will balance the remaining karma at the astral level, which allows us to start from scratch. After this cleaning of our slate, we follow all instructions from our master; thus, no new karma gets created.

Again, this statement comes from spiritual literature. The issue is not as simple. After initiation, we do not change to the extent that we suddenly become a saint. We are still the same person, with the same desires, feelings of greed and attachments. The process of cleaning ourselves from these feelings is lengthy and complicated. We can be aware of very high spiritual levels while at the same time experiencing the desire to obtain goods at the material level of awareness. The mind keeps on challenging us, and we do not want to become consciously aware of the nameless until we are clean. My statement refers to us; nobody stops us from entering the nameless. Until we balance our feelings, we do not desire to enter the nameless.

Why would we forfeit all these pleasant feelings and enter something that we can only describe as "Nothing"?

It is this simple. There is no physical guard that stops us. There is only us, and we do not want to go until we are ready.

Before we continue to the spiritual path and its components, we need to deal with the human way of communication and the subject of coincidences.

-oOo-

The Concept of Communication

I wrote about this subject before, but it needs dealing with again to complement this book's contents. The reason is that everything I wrote is a form of communication, and people can only convey items they feel are essential via a communication tool they understand. Rather than referring to the limitations of outward communication methods, I add the story as a chapter in this book.

-oOo-

Any entity that lives at the material level of awareness cannot communicate properly. We always require some form of interface to allow understanding by our mind. The body contains several tools that enable comprehension of its environment; we refer to these tools as senses. Apart from the material senses, most entities can communicate via feelings. Humans suppressed communication via feelings due to their use of a language.

A few of the entities living on mother earth mastered a simplistic way to produce complicated sounds, which have a meaning. Humanity proudly claims that their way of communicating via sounds in the outside world is the most proficient. We call this complex system of sounds a language. We even managed to make little drawings related to each of these sounds; we call this writing. We ignore entirely that proper communication at the material level of awareness is the passing on of feelings. We also forget that direct communication at the material awareness level between humans is not possible. Humans use the mouth as a tool to communicate, but we still need to use the mind as another interface even when we use feelings.

The design of our communication system has flaws:

As the sounds we designed refer to feelings, it is possible, and we have proof of this, that the communication of what we want to convey does not happen properly.

When humans are not in touch for a relatively short period, the sounds related to a particular aspect of feelings change, and we fail to understand each other. Depending on the time between meetings and the difference in sounds, we refer to a dialect or another language.

We can produce sounds to convey a purposely incorrect message, i.e., not related to the feeling. We call this type of communication lying.

When we use a language, we can only communicate with other humans, and even this communication is limited.

Due to our reliance on this type of communication, we expect other entities to master this as well. We regard our capability as a sign of superiority over other living entities. When we look for life on other planets, we try to detect this outward way of communicating. We call this a sign that an adequately developed civilisation exists.

The Bible identifies the issue of human communication by telling the allegorical story of the tower of Babel. In this story, God punishes humanity for trying to build a tower to reach heaven. God introduced the concept of languages, and humans could not understand each other anymore. Consequently, the tower of Babel never got completed because people could not communicate. We can explain this story as follows:

Proper communication at the material level of awareness happens via the use of feelings. At some stage, humanity lived like all other life in the world, communicating with each other by using feelings. However, this communication method has its limitations. When we need to build something, we need to prepare a design, we need drawings and written text, and we need to communicate this information to a building team. To achieve this, humans developed language and writing. Designing the concept of speech and committing the speech to paper resulted from this outward way of trying to live our lives. Creating a language, including a written version, is a simplistic alternative for proper communication. These forms of communication are not direct and are open to various forms of abuse, as we mentioned before.

Of course, we can refer to all our achievements that occurred. These happened because we have the tools of language and writing. We would never have achieved what we made from this world without these developments.

What have we achieved?

Consider the reason for us being at this material level of awareness. We do not know how to learn one of the essential things in our lives. We would love to live in the NOW, in the present. All our gurus tell us that this is the only way to live. But we can never live in the present because we speak, we write. Our precious language and our writing stop us from living in the present.

How can we live in the present when we think with words? We can, of course, take an example from the plants and animals. We can learn from all other life on this earth. We can go back to the moment that we lost the proper way of communicating at the material awareness level. However, looking at what goes on in the world, we may be too late to change direction. We cannot join up with other life on this planet and learn to live our lives in heaven; live our lives in the present. We have chosen a challenging path to spiritual progress. We now must find our way back to the main road. We must find the way back; we must return to the main path in life, else we may well destroy this road for all life on this planet forever.

As humans, we have forsaken the natural way of communicating as given to us by design. The punishment is that we have a vastly inadequate communication system. The penalty is, of course, related to what we have produced ourselves. God does not punish anybody; we are very capable of doing this job ourselves. As long as we consider that we designed a proper communication system, we will not communicate correctly.

Communication is not the only issue with the way humanity lives their lives. As mentioned before, the material world is an illusion. The mind created this as an alternative for reality, which is to merge in the nameless. Humanity invented a lot to copy the mind's creations, and their designs are nowhere near as impressive as nature. All we did was attaching us more to the mind's illusions and slow our progress on the path to our final destination.

-o0o-

When we discuss communication, we should mention non-verbal communication as well, as this, in most cases, is more relevant than our language. Nonverbal communication gets nearer to what proper communication should be like, as it relates to our feelings. However, this way of communicating is generally very sub-conscious. Another limitation of non-verbal communication is that it relies mainly on the eyes and our limbs' movement. Although nearer to our feelings, it still requires this external interface.

The forms of communication that humans developed always involve the body in some way. They are, therefore, indirect and use the outside path. There are more direct forms of communication, where people are known to convey feelings to each other. Identical twins often can feel what the other twin experiences, but generally, we cannot communicate directly. We mostly do not even believe that direct communication is possible. The way we receive our initial instruction and education in life causes this perception.

A human being has the capability of communicating relatively direct. However, we are taught from our early years onward to learn to use the complicated and outward way of producing sounds; our tutors force us to master a language. The result is that any other communication ability we have has been rendered dormant. We do know that other forms of communication exist. We do not believe that these methods are effective;

anyhow, these systems are only for a selected few. Our trusted language based on complicated sounds is – in our view – the best way to communicate, and it sets us apart from all other life on this planet.

I specifically do not use the term "puts us above", as many people believe it is reality. It is my view that language is one of the worst things that happened to the human race. We can communicate directly with other humans, but our education never included developing this skill. The result is that we are doomed to communicate with complicated sounds, which is an outward and flawed way of communication.

Can we reverse this process?

Of course, it is possible to reverse what we have done, but this will take a few generations. We do not have proper teachers, and we need to teach parents to teach their children something that they do not know themselves. Humans have achieved impossible tasks before, and, therefore, I am confident that we accomplish this task at some stage, but we have to wait for the right time. The present system of education is moving towards teaching children from young onward to express feelings. This reverse in our educational system is a good start, and when followed through, our children will become very different from the way we behave.

How is this story relevant?

A seeker should start the process of opening up toward feelings. We may find this problematic because it for sure leads to friends and family issues, as the initial opening up can lead to friction in relationships. The exercises below are more straightforward for women, but men can learn from this by admitting that they must work harder in the learning process than the average woman.

Men will have to work harder at developing feelings because, in Western culture, men are encouraged from birth onward not to express emotions. In other cultures, this situation is slightly different, but, even in these cultures, the difference between men and women is that women will find it easier to develop their feelings.

The exercises below are a start, and as soon as people start developing their feelings, they will also create routines that are much more effective. However, we have to start somewhere.

1)

When we have to make a decision, first listen to what our gut feeling recommends. Only after this start the thinking process. Make sure you give as much priority to the gut feeling as is reasonably possible. Often – primarily men – take decisions based on logical reasoning. Feelings are for older women! A statement like this should not have a place in our vocabulary, and we should always give preference to feelings.

2)

Discuss any issues you have with people you trust. Find as many people you trust as you can and make it a point to discuss things you usually would class as private. Challenge anything that you class as private. Find out what you consider to be confidential, and challenge the reason for doing this. We should not have anything classed as personal or secret. It leads to dishonesty and is a way to create power over others. When we learn to communicate via feelings, the concept of privacy and confidentiality will disappear.

3)
When you love people, tell them that you love them in no uncertain terms. Do not hold back; you love a friend, say so and why. What this means is that we must learn to differentiate between love and attraction. This differentiation must be made clear in the way we express ourselves. We do not want to lose friends based on this issue. We can love people, and we can have the desire to have sex with somebody. These are two different types of feelings, and the way we express them should make it clear which option we mean.

4)
When we feel the need to cry, do so. Do not hold this feeling back because others are watching. When a story or a film makes you cry, let the tears openly flow, and be proud that you can do this. The statement that a man does not cry or show his feelings is outdated, and we should distance ourselves from such an opinion. For a man, this isn't easy, as our education told us to think differently. However, we should realise the reason for educating men like this; the objective was to create people who work without complaining. Tears and questions do not fit in that educational pattern. Break the pattern. Not easy, but it needs doing.

5)
When you are happy and excited about something, show the world! Dance if you feel like it. Studies show that people who can show

their feelings live longer. I do not know how they scientifically established this, but they did it, so let us go for it.

The above exercises are relatively simple, but for those that have suppressed their feelings for a lifetime, these exercises can prove to be complicated. Try it out and make it a habit to follow the suggestions. We need to get our feelings to the surface of our consciousness, not suppressed in our sub-consciousness.

We need to progress on the path to becoming aware of the totality of consciousness. Therefore, the exercises are a requirement. We need to be able to communicate with feelings. Without this comprehension, the step to the spiritual level will be difficult.

As coincidences are an essential part of the communication from the higher levels of our consciousness, we deal with this in the next chapter.

-o0o-

Coincidences

People consider that a lot happens in their lives, which they cannot explain. Since humans came to exist in the world, they looked for explanations of why unfortunate events happen. They refer to such events as bad luck. In some cases, they look at their Gods and regard the events as a punishment. For some reason, situations that people could consider lucky get a lot less attention. People tend to look for something to blame, and we do not need to attach blame to winning the lottery!

-oOo-

Nothing in our life happens by accident. What we call good luck or bad luck is all part of the theatre of life, and our self orchestrated this somewhere at the higher awareness levels of our consciousness before we got born. As we cannot comprehend why certain events happen to us, we give it a name and call it a coincidence. Luck, bad luck, chance or a coincidence fall under a strictly controlled system called: 'The Law of Coincidence.' The law of coincidence ensures that we meet everything we need to encounter during the soul's development.

As the soul is inherently a perfect entity, why does it require development?

To be part of the ocean we refer to as the nameless, the soul needs to shed its attachments and desires. When an out of balance feeling occurs, this part automatically separates itself from the nameless and starts its journey from the bottom upwards. Again, we note that there are no high-level entities involved in this decision. A part of the nameless decides to be a single entity. By taking this path, it automatically creates an unbalance and distances itself as an entity. When this happens, this part, which constitutes the soul, needs to decide how to enter the material level. The soul makes such a decision based on its desires.

When we refer to educating the soul, we mean that the soul needs to recognise that all its experiences are an illusion. When this recognition occurs, the soul knows that it wants to return to its home, the ocean of balanced energy that we refer to as the nameless. Until the realisation happens, the soul will enjoy its existence at the immeasurable number of awareness levels. It needs to learn that even awareness is an attachment. Only when it knows this will it start its return to the nameless.

-o0o-

After explaining the reason for the soul's development, we can now define how it progresses.

All events that happen in our life are experiences that the soul requires for its development. Initially, the soul designs these experiences to create the satisfaction of its desires. It loves to emerge in the pleasures generated by the mind. The soul does not realise that it all amounts to an illusion, which the mind created to further the material body's satisfaction. When the realisation starts, the soul takes more control and attempts to steer the body to cause a return to its home.

To steer our body at the material awareness level, we require some form of communication. However, the dimension of time is not relevant to the soul. Being mainly at the spiritual awareness level, the soul needs to convey messages that the material body can understand. The soul does this in three ways:

> A flash of knowledge comes to us.
> A coincidence happens in our lives.
> A feeling occurs that guides us in a direction.

An ordinary human cannot comprehend anything that does not contain the dimension of time. The mind created time to render all that happens around us understandable. Also, the concept of "understanding" relates to the mind. We will be using words to bring this to a level of understanding. The soul's development relates to its learning to assume the role of being the driver of events. The process of becoming aware can be immediate, or it can take many lives. Eventually, this is not important. What is essential is that the soul does not get diverted to the mind's distractions during the learning process.

A seeker needs to grasp the process and understand the communications from the soul. Maybe this appears simple, but for a start, our design contains the mind, and therefore, the dimension of time. How to cope with the disparity between the way the soul operates and the way we work?

There is one way that we will get anywhere near to understanding what happens when the dimension of time does not exist, and that is to attempt to live in the present. Living in the present is not identical – we compare the factor "stopped time" with the element "no time". However, it will give us at least an impression of what this concept means. For this reason, guru's in the past and the present-day tell us to live in the NOW.

When we do, we experience life without the past and the future. When we achieve this, we will get a little bit of comprehension of what it is like to exist without the limitations of the dimension of time. It can never be a complete understanding; the word "understanding" requires the use of the mind. Living in the present consciously for any amount of time while maintaining full awareness of what we do is not easy. I consider this option, therefore, more of a theoretical possibility.

-o0o-

How do we translate the possibility of understanding coincidences into concrete action?

We cannot execute the communication between the higher awareness levels of our consciousness and the material awareness level by using words, as these are unique to the material awareness level. The way the higher awareness levels of our consciousness communicate is direct, which the material awareness level cannot understand. That leads to the question: "How do we communicate between the various levels?"

There appear to be several ways:

When we are very involved with a subject – any subject – and the involvement requires answers or action, at times, we stop the thinking process. Ideas will come to us, and these originate from the higher awareness levels of our consciousness. This system works for thoughts and ideas, but it also works for action. A painter can and will use this when painting. The painter creates feeling into the painting this way. A writer can exploit this, which is the awareness level where the writer's real ideas originate. Any feeling in any activity will somehow come from the higher awareness levels of our consciousness.

The mind at the material level of our consciousness cannot produce real feelings and creativity. The more we practice the feeling way of living, the more we will see ideas coming to us. When we use this approach, we find that these feelings even influence how we live our lives.

This communication method works well. However, the soul is still fully content with its existence at the material awareness level. When we become conscious of the need for spiritual development, the soul is ready, and we can use the method for our progression.

In our life, we meet situations which appear to be by accident. When we try to analyse the possibility of these coincidences happening, we find that the chance of such an occurrence happening is tiny. We call these moments coincidences, and generally, we believe that this happens by accident, and we call it a bit of luck or bad luck. The issue with a chance is that it has to happen evenly towards luck and bad luck. I like to quote to you a story described by the psychiatrist Jung, but put it in my own words:

During the psychiatric treatment of an intelligent woman, Jung found that he could not get through to her because of her high intelligence level. He was on the border of giving up, but one day when he asked her about a dream, she described having seen a golden beetle, a scarab. These insects do exist in Germany, but they are scarce. When she talked about her dream, Jung heard a knocking, and when he opened the window, a golden beetle flew in. Jung told the woman: 'here is your beetle!' The woman was distraught, as she knew that the chance of such an event happening was unbelievably slight, and her mind could not comprehend and explain this very rare coincidence. After this incident, treatment could be affected.

Jung firmly believed in the concept of the law of coincidences, and he wrote somewhere that when tabulated, coincidences are more positive than negative, which he statistically could not explain. Jung, therefore, believed that the concept of karma must have some truth in it. I have no idea why Jung brought the idea of karma to the equation.

I found that when we tune in to the possibility of coincidences, we see them happening more frequently. It appears that we have a communication channel that goes from the top down in our consciousness. Whether there is also a possibility to communicate with the material awareness level to higher awareness levels is not clear to me. Spiritual literature informs us that such a communication method does not exist.

I have read a statement from a master that communication is only possible from high to low, but being an engineer by profession, I like to find proof for such information. When reading up, I only find books explaining how to receive communications from the higher levels. The books from Cyndi Dale are proof of this and what she teaches appears to work.

The main message that I can give here is that we have to be open to coincidences as they are part of the communication channel with our consciousness's higher awareness levels. To tune in to these coincidences, we must be very aware of what goes on around us.

Ultimately, everything that happens in our life has a meaning, but it takes a lot of wisdom to interpret every event that occurs during our existence.

-oOo-

We will now relate the concept of coincidences to energy, as this is what we do in this book.

At some stage during our development, the soul knows that it is time to return to its proper home. To achieve this, it needs to take control of the body and steer it to become aware of our consciousness's totality. Up until that time, the soul was happy to let the material body take its decisions and let events develop as planned at the physical level. We can show our decision making in a simplistic format as follows.

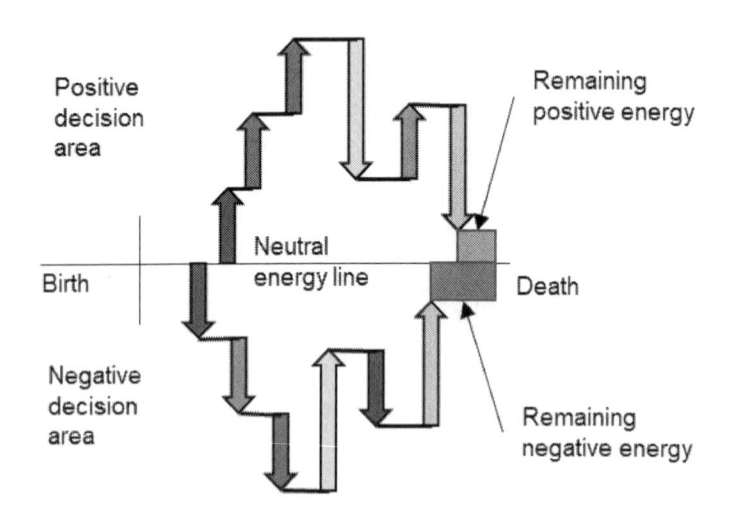

The drawing shows that we make decisions, and karma compensation or opposing energy follows later. By then, we made other decisions; thus, the chance to end up with a zero energy balance is tiny.

When the soul takes control of our lives, it will guide our body at the material level of awareness. The soul will execute the control by adding the correct type of energy at the right time, and we will react to this.

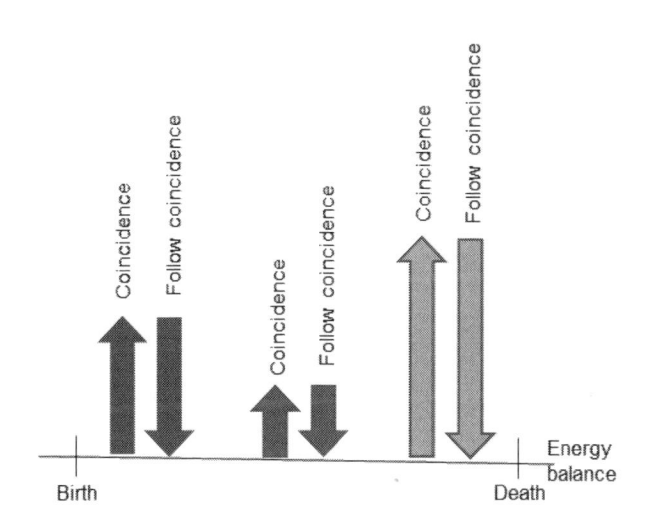

In the picture, we can see that the soul creates a coincidence. The soul does this by creating an intention, which our consciousness and mind translate into an event at the material awareness level; we call this a coincidence. Such an event causes a deviation from the energy-neutral line, but when we decide to act upon the event, the decision to act will reverse the energy unbalance. Following a coincidence does not involve the dimension of time as the soul is involved. We see now that when we start following the coincidences, the energy balance will stay neutral; we will not create karma as we follow the inner master. When we read about the disciple following the master at all times, this is the meaning of this statement.

We make around 60,000 decisions each day, so following the soul's guidance is essential to keep the energy balance at zero. When we follow coincidences, our mind and consciousness will realise that we do not create any more karma. Because of this, they, together, create an event to release the surplus karma. This event constitutes meeting a master who can balance the energy levels to zero and guide us through the spiritual awareness levels to return to our home.

This story is, of course, quite simplistic. There is ample proof that people meet their outside master before they are completely ready. There is also abundant proof that following a master does not render the disciple prepared, even though the master thinks the disciple is fully prepared. However, the overall intention of the story provides the ideal way life should develop.

A natural follow up to coincidences is to discuss spiritual experiences.

-o0o-

Spiritual Experiences

When we start on the path to full awareness, one of the first things we may experience is unique feelings that we regard as abnormal; i.e. not related to anything we know from the collected memories of our material existence. We refer to these events as spiritual experiences.

Such experiences relate to coincidences, and they signify that the soul starts taking control of the machinery we call "our body".

-oOo-

When we execute real meditation, we may get experiences that appear to be spiritual. Be always careful; such experiences can also be a creation of the mind rather than genuine spiritual experiences.

A few questions spring to mind, each of which I will answer in this chapter.

> What are spiritual experiences?
> Why does the mind try to copy these experiences?
> How can we tell the difference?

Let me first define the concept of a spiritual experience:

A spiritual experience is any contact we have with the higher levels of our consciousness.

Although this sounds like a proper and straightforward definition, interference by the mind does make detection difficult. To arrive anywhere near a logical process, we first need to define what the mind does and what it tries to achieve. The mind has an essential job during spiritual development; it needs to ensure that our soul is ready to progress. It does this with the tools it has available; these are the five vices:

Anger
Greed
Attachment
Lust
Ego

The physical domain

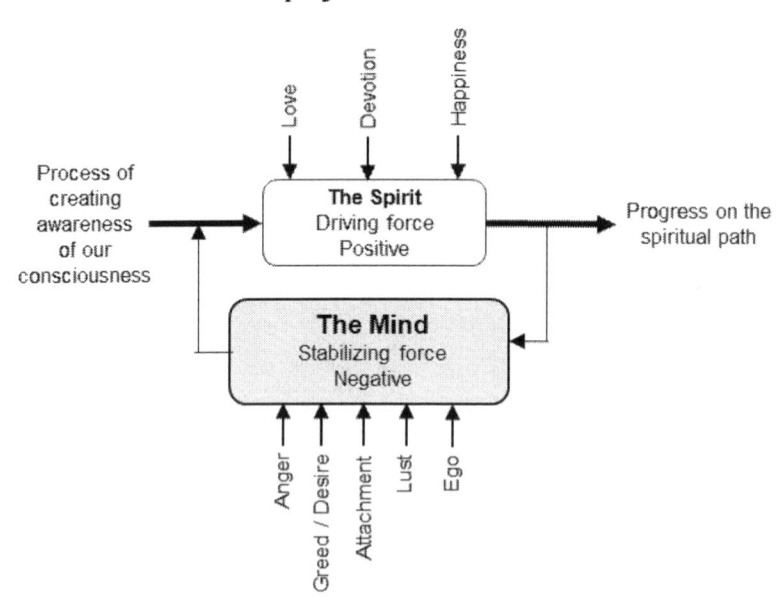

```
Process of creating awareness of our consciousness  →  The Spirit
                                                        Driving force
                                                        Positive         →  Progress on the spiritual path

                                                      The Mind
                                                      Stabilizing force
                                                      Negative

Inputs to Spirit: Love, Devotion, Happiness
Inputs to Mind: Anger, Greed / Desire, Attachment, Lust, Ego
```

In a previous book, I used the drawing above to make this clear. I had to make a few modifications, but the essence is the same; spiritual development is a control system with a driving force and a stabilising force.

Humanity claims to have invented the concept of control systems. However, the reality is that nature at the physical awareness level operates with these systems, and we have recently discovered the intricacy of its workings.

To follow the drawing: At the physical awareness level, by using our attention, we attempt to focus on the discovery of our consciousness. However, the five vices push the mind to distract us from this aim. The spirit moves us forward, using its tools of love, devotion and happiness. The five vices try to copy these feelings and make these illusions as attractive as possible to distract us from achieving progress. The result is that we follow the path of spiritual progress, but our movement gets slowed down to create stability. The vices are, therefore, simple controls. They are not good or bad; they follow their assigned task. When we cannot control these vices and stop our progress, we should not blame the controls. We need to learn to operate the complex machinery we call our body.

I always try to compare this with driving a car. By using the steering wheel, we continuously adjust direction, and this constant adjustment keeps us on the road. When we try to keep the steering wheel in one position, we find that the car will go off the road. Positive and negative adjustments are a requirement. We also need to use the brakes and the throttle. By only using the throttle's forward force, we will eventually crash the car as the speed gets too high.

-oOo-

The obvious way that the mind can lure us to the material awareness level is to produce beautiful experiences. These always relate to our senses; we see and hear something fantastic. Be aware that spiritual progress is not a circus – a quote from Vivekananda. He was correct; anything to do with the senses originates from the mind and the five vices, as the awareness levels past the mind's domain do not rely on a body. Therefore, the utilisation of senses will not be a factor. We have to learn to enjoy higher awareness levels. These are very subtle, and initially, one can wonder what the fuss is all about. Only when we pursue our goal will the attraction become apparent, and we will realise that the rather crude way the mind tries to copy these is nowhere near reality.

When we focus our attention past the mind's domain, we may assume that all is now well, and we can forget about the mind and its vices. The drawing below shows a different picture.

The spiritual domain

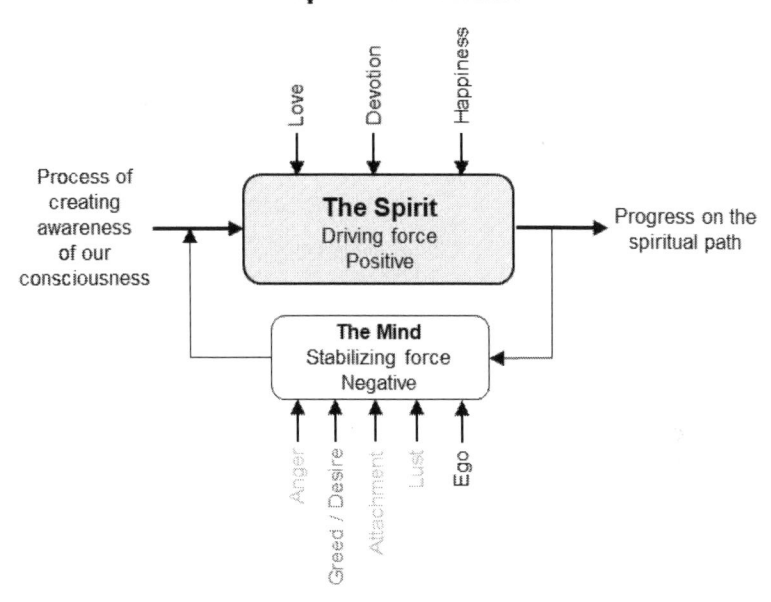

By making the spirit box larger and adding the fill colour, I indicated the increased influence. However, the mind still has some effect> I showed this by changing the colours to shades of grey. The ego is still entirely black, while Desire has a more significant impact. Even those that manage to focus their awareness at the spiritual level must be careful not to fall for the mind's influence. Again, the objective is to create a stabilising force, slow progress until the soul can detect the distinction between illusion and reality. When we progress, the spirit's influence becomes more pronounced, but the combination of being advanced and the capabilities that come with this can lure the seeker back to the attractions created by the mind. The mind never gives up; it keeps the seeker on its toes by creating diversions that are difficult to resist.

-o0o-

To distinguish between experiences, I study any of the experiences that happen to me. If they occur in front of me, outside my body, they are related to the mind, as they are external. When something happens at the third eye point in my head, they relate to a spiritual experience. When I started doing this, based on Ishwar Puri's suggestion, all my experiences disappeared, and all that I encountered was the colour black. To counter the mind's attempts to show beautiful colours and shapes and push back the thinking process was exceedingly difficult. To sort this out, the process of meditation became a great help.

Of course, we may have a spiritual experience at the material level of awareness, like a message from our intuition level. Such messages come as a flash, sometimes referred to as insight. One moment we do not know how to continue; the next moment, we know as clear as daylight the path forward. Do we class this as a spiritual experience? Yes, but it belongs at the physical levels of awareness, although it originated from the spirit level of awareness. Such flashes are guidance from the higher levels of our consciousness. They inform us how life should proceed.

Spiritual literature tells us that this is what happens, and I agree. We do encounter a contradiction. If our actions at the material awareness level are predetermined at the astral level before we got born, how do we make this contradiction understandable? We can refuse to follow the messages, and most people do. We will deal with this issue later. For now, we list typical experiences and come to an explanation of why they occur, and what it means.

Attention to events in nature:

Once I noticed a flock of birds flying near the ground, moving very fast in a perfect square, continuously. I had never seen such behaviour before, and I looked on in astonishment. Such an experience happens because we meditate and keep our attention focused on the third eye. The event is likely not uncommon, but our perception of the creation around us becomes more explicit; more focused. It is the result of our spiritual efforts, but in itself, it is not a spiritual experience. However, it is a sign that we become aware of the astral regions.

When walking in a forest, the trees appear to generate a feeling, and different trees generate different emotions. Such feelings are the result of meditation exercises and are a spiritual experience related to the astral region. We require such events and feelings to happen to show us our progress. The art of focusing our attention is difficult to achieve, as we did not start this at a young age. When we reach this focus, we experience events like this at the material level of our awareness.

When we look at any plant, we suddenly feel a unique personality, even if someone pruned the plant into an exact shape. Each plant appears different and unique. In a way, we access the astral region; else, we would not see this. We can class this as a spiritual experience. However, it belongs firmly on the outside path of our development.

When sitting relaxed, looking at people, we suddenly notice that all these people are content with their existence. They may, on the outside, look angry or happy or upset, but they fit in. Feeling this generates an excellent feeling inside us. Seeing the people in itself is not a spiritual experience, but the feeling we experience is love and is a spiritual experience.

We can sit relaxed in the sun, thinking about nothing, and feel very happy. The experience can be of such a strength that we do not let go, leading to a bad sunburn. In a way, this is a spiritual experience. Any feeling of happiness should be spiritual, although it relates to the outside path.

Walking sideways:
This effect happens to some of us when we concentrate intensely. It is an experience related to the astral region and a spiritual experience on the outside path.

-oOo-

All the examples generated show either that they are not a spiritual experience or an outside path experience. We may, therefore, wonder what we experience when we enter the inside path. The easy answer is that nothing we experience at the material awareness level relates to the inside path. Our capabilities, our senses, do not reach out to these levels, and the best that we can state is that we experience "Nothing".

Any experience that does not relate to something they have ever met before is disturbing to the extreme to ordinary people. I mentioned Khalil Gibran before and his poem "The Madman". His opinion is that when we remove all the masks that people create in their lives, they become madmen. Now imagine that we lose all the adjustments we made to the way we live during our life; we also enter a completely and utterly alien world as to what we are used to at the material level of awareness. Such an experience may render us insane. We may have hit now the reason for slowing spiritual progress; we need preparation to enter this new experience. The mind generates material equivalents to prepare us for these experiences,

Of course, this explanation is, like everything, just a simplistic guess of what goes on. We cannot point out the exact system as it got designed. The complexity is too high to comprehend. However, I would not be an engineer if I did not give the challenge a serious try.

When we go past the jump to the region of the spirit, everything we experience is black. We see it like this because we do not use our senses, and we need to say something. Being engulfed in blackness can be disturbing. The tendency is to open one's eyes and forget meditation, as the experience of this blackness goes with a scary feeling that is difficult to define.

When we persist in this region, we will experience the blackness to start moving; we feel claustrophobic in this moving blackness like we feel in the absolute darkness of a cave. We go now through the experience of the wirling cave. Only after we force ourselves through these experiences will we slowly get accustomed to all these experiences, and we start feeling very much at home. We now feel what actual love means and the experience of being at home. From this moment onward, we exist in the pure spirit part of our consciousness.

The mind's influence is still apparent, as we are separate. However, the feeling of love and devotion, plus the effect of the audible lifestream, is so strong that the mind has little chance to pull us back to the material level awareness. However, it can happen, and it has happened.

When we move our awareness to the nameless, there is no explanation and experience; we disappear into all that exists. However, we still have all the experiences of the lower parts of our consciousness, including our material body. When we can be aware of all aspects of our consciousness, Eastern belief systems refer to such a person as perfect and a saint. However, like everything else in the material world, these terms are often awarded as an honorary title, which means that we cannot rely on selecting such a person as a teacher.

To reach every awareness level of our consciousness, we need assistance from such a person; this is the lesson we learn from Sant Mat teachers.

The lessons are in contradiction with reality. The likelihood of somebody being this far advanced is small; estimates range that at any one time, we have one to eight of these people in the world. How can the world develop when this amount of people have to serve billions in need?

The incompatibility of these numbers we deal with in the chapter about masters. In the previous chapter, we mentioned the astral level of awareness as the first level we reach after learning to focus our awareness on our consciousness. For this reason, it is a significant level, and I created a separate chapter on the subject.

-oOo-

The Astral level of Awareness

We discussed all awareness levels of our consciousness and the existence of personalities. However, the astral level is for most of us on the spiritual path special, as it is the only awareness level that we can easily reach. To ensure that we know what this means, we created this chapter.

During our meditation exercises, we find that when we live with our attention focused continuously on the third eye, we become more aware. We notice this because the world becomes more alive, and we see and experience everything around us more vivid. Such experiences are the first stages of entering the astral regions. Eventually, we may find that we move out of our body via a hole in our forehead between the eyebrows. Alternatively, we may find that we stand up while our body is still sitting in meditation. It does not matter; all experiences like this mean that we enter the lower astral awareness levels.

Most meditation systems teach people to reach these levels, and they often regard achieving the highest astral level as being in heaven. They assume that they do not require further development. The highest astral level is quite an experience, and at this level, we, apparently, can meet with the souls of special people we heard about from the past. Surely we are now in heaven?

The stories are clear enough, but what does it mean in Western terminology?

-o0o-

The astral level of awareness consists of our body's senses without the material body's ballast. We can experience this level by executing meditation exercises. Achieving these awareness levels without assistance is possible. Contrary to some stories, the astral region's awareness is a range of levels, each with a slightly better experience than the level below. The astral level consists of entire worlds, and it is like the material universe, without the involvement of matter. As it is under the control of the mind, the astral level is build up from personalities. What some religions call God is the overarching personality of the astral level of awareness. Although seen as an extraordinary personality, this entity is nowhere near what a seeker intends to achieve when following the path to total awareness. However, the creator of the astral region is a powerful entity.

Eastern philosophy knows this entity, and they gave it a name. I removed all names of personalities from this book, as it would take a lot of study to identify each one of them, and I likely will forget some. As far as knowledge goes, knowing of their existence is sufficient. There is no need for a seeker to try to comprehend lots of difficult names. Eventually, all these personalities amount to energy in vibration, separating parts, and creating other parts. Some of these entities are more prominent than others, depending on their place on the ladder of consciousness. When we comprehend the totality, we will understand and know who they are.

Any seeker who wishes to know more about this should study the Sikh religion and Hindu and Buddhist philosophies. Each of these looks at slightly different concepts and realities, but the information is available. I recommend, as before, obtaining a copy of The Path of the Masters. It gives an excellent introduction to all a seeker needs to know.

-o0o-

To reach the astral level, we meditate with our attention concentrated on the third eye. Most descriptions of this level come from Eastern monks and yogis. These people often do not know about the sound current, and they assume that they reach the ultimate destination because of all the beauty they encounter. However, when we reach the actual spiritual levels, the term beautiful and magnificent are not relevant. These terms relate to our senses, and we do not use our senses after leaving the physical levels behind.

I mentioned this before, but when we, during meditation, encounter many beautiful colours, try to locate the experience with our hand. Likely, it is in front of our head. The experience may then relate to the astral level, but it is not part of the inner path. The inner path to the spiritual regions will not use our senses; thus, anything we regard as an experience is an illusion. We need to learn to experience without the use of the astral body.

Yogananda once said that the spiritual path is not a circus. He indicated that we should not expect everything to be beautiful in the material awareness sense. Pleasing our senses is not the objective of progress on the spiritual path. The real aim is to reach above the spiritual level and achieve merging in "Nothing". Before we unite with the nameless, we will experience lots of awareness levels. Initially, these are all part of the astral plane. There is so much to feel and to see; we love to stay and enjoy the experience.

We should realise that we are on the outer path, and it is the mind translating the energy works into a visual show. It constitutes an illusion, meant to keep us hooked to the level we are at; the mind creates an attachment. As long as we give in to the illusion, we will not move on; we stay put. Nothing wrong with this, but to make spiritual progress, we must keep on working on our meditation exercises and keep away from the beautiful illusions created by the mind.

The word "experience" refers to the outer path and creations of the mind. When we see lovely lights and colours, it should be evident that this relates to the senses of our material awareness level. My advice is to expect nothing and continue to pursue following the path while experiencing not a thing. Eventually, results become apparent.

Julian Johnson describes the top of the astral levels as a powerhouse of lights. It is difficult to find out what we really should expect when exploring our consciousness. My suggestion is that we should aim for no experience. Any time we experience something, test the event by locating its place. When it is outside our head, it is an outer experience, not related to the spiritual path. It took me quite a while to keep my attention on the third eye for a prolonged period, and it crushed all experiences that I found comforting and beautiful. The initial feeling I had was darkness, but after some time, that gives way to other emotions, which are more delightful.

To progress through to the astral regions, we act as follows: We imagine sitting in a room inside our head, between our ears while being level with a point between our brows. Everything that we experience should be from this point. Do not give in to colours or lights; I found these always happening in front of my head. Engage with the person in your head, but keep on being in that place.

Progress will happen, but give it time. People told me that they work a lot, but they do not experience anything. The lesson is that "Nothing", eventually, is the best experience we can encounter. All the beautiful colours of the astral region are a way to distract us from reaching spiritual awareness levels. When we work, we will progress. Avoid feeling discouraged and sad. These feelings are detrimental to progress. The art is not to expect anything, just meditate and learn to exercise during our everyday activities. We will slowly improve our awareness. Do not expect to jump suddenly into another world; the spiritual path does not operate in this way.

-oOo-

The astral awareness level is the place where we decide about our life at the material level. Our astral body moves out of the material body when we pass away. It takes with it all our awareness, and it goes to one of the astral areas. When our attachment to the material world is powerful, we will not even go very far. We are in a dark and frightening place, which increases our desire to return to the material level. All our memories are strong at this level, and these will confront us. The combination of fright, memories, and desires led to the stories about demons and black angels that punish us before we return. A seeker should realise that we will encounter awareness levels like this, and we should ensure that we move on and do not get hooked on the presence of entities in these regions. The experience can be frightening.

Those who meditated sufficiently to access the astral awareness levels before they pass away know what to experience, and they will handle the situation. They know how to recognise their inner guide and be guided to the location they need to reach. Their desires will eventually stop them, and depending on where they are in the ranking of personalities, their astral body will return to the material level of awareness.

When we hear about re-incarnation, this is how it works. Our material body never returns to the material world; it will go to dust. But our awareness and desires will return. The combination of the legacy of our previous lives determines what life we lead next. Higher Lords and Gods do not decide anything that happens to us; we decide everything that occurs in our lives by ourselves.

When we enter the spiritual awareness levels, returning to the material awareness level becomes optional. The pull of the mind is still apparent, but we are now at such an advanced state that we can choose. Such a choice we make based on a desire to experience the pleasures again, but some feel that – by their return – they can assist others in moving up to total awareness. Eventually, it does not matter. Our final goal is to merge in the nameless. Any reason for a return to lower levels has its base in longing for its pleasures. We should admire those that achieve this level of awareness, but to progress, we must also be aware of the pitfalls and the reasons for the stops on the path.

-o0o-

The astral awareness level precedes the causal awareness level. Very few people achieve these awareness levels. The perception is that special monks and those we regard as holy persons reach high awareness, as they are near to God. Such assumptions are not correct. Any person who gets to a high level of visibility at the material awareness level is likely very attached to this level. Otherwise, why work hard to achieve such a celebrity status? I presume that we can achieve the status without wishing this to happen, but when we study people, mostly when people are visible, they worked hard to gain such visibility.

We can learn a lot from people like this, but to meet somebody who is a spiritual master who can help us reach our consciousness's spiritual levels, we may need to be careful. To get higher than the astral region, we need to be aware of the audible lifestream, and we need to receive some form of instruction on how to train our inner ear to hear this enchanting sound. We deal with this subject in the next chapter, as it is an essential subject to continue our progress in our spiritual development.

-o0o-

The Audible Lifestream

The term audible lifestream is around at the spiritual level, but what does it mean when explained by an engineering mind?

All matter finds its origin in vibrating energy. Those who studied spirituality in the past and present believe this and our scientists know this as well. Simple physics tells us that matter is not as stable as we think it is. Matter consists of particles that hang in what, up to now, gets classed as emptiness. These particles vibrate, and a strong force holds them into place. The empty area accounts for over 99% of all matter. By studying the particles, we identified many different sorts, but there is a commonality; they all are vibrating energy. They can interchange, which means that one can become another. Physics dictates that any vibration needs matter to be the underlying base, i.e. no vibration occurs when there is no matter. The exception to this law is light, which vibrates even in space where there is no matter. Spiritual belief is that space is never empty; it contains static energy, which becomes a form of matter when brought into vibration.

Science and spirituality do not appear to be too far apart; what needs explaining is the reason for the vibration and its source. Something causes the vibration, and that something sustains it, as the movement does not stop.

Spirituality teaches us that everything we know contains a sound, referred to as the audible lifestream or by some as the sound current. We use both names in this book, but the vibration is only at the lower levels of our awareness perceived as a sound.

A lot more descriptions are around in various languages, but using the terms audible lifestream and sound current for this book is sufficient. This sound current makes everything vibrate. It is not an assumption that is impossible to prove; when we train ourselves sufficiently, we will detect this audible lifestream as a sound. We cannot hear it with the ears we use at the material level of awareness, but with some simple meditation training, we can learn to detect this vibration as a sound.

Initially, this will be a buzz. When we progress, we find that within this buzzing, a melodic sound emerges. What happens is that we tune in to a specific spectrum of the buzz. Depending on which area of our consciousness we enter, this melodic sound has different frequencies.

The sound we experience is the audible lifestream that permeates the whole of the creation. As long as we merge in the material awareness level only, we tend to look for where this sound originates from; we search for its source. However, there is no beginning, and there is no end. The tune is everywhere, and it is so beautiful; we cannot copy or describe it. It is the vibration that keeps everything in existence.

-o0o-

Before we discuss this vibration source, we first want to explain why it comes over as exceedingly beautiful.

People have a perception of everything that occurs around them. We do not know what exactly happens; we can only detect what is within our senses' capability. Scientifically, we know that our capacity to detect is exceedingly limited, but we can extend our ability to detect with the appropriate tools. However, our original perception tends to cloud our knowledge. As discussed above, scientific studies show us that matter consists of mostly space with some particles of vibrating energy. Even some scientists wrote that although most of what we perceive to be matter consist of vibrating energy in space, there is also some real matter. When I read this, I wondered what they found that justified this statement.

What we perceive as beautiful is anything special to us. Using this logic, a vibration that created us and kept us alive is the most special, and we perceive this sound as the most beautiful. The audible lifestream at the material level is like the sound of a conch or a bell. As happens with all descriptions, without the concept's experience, an explanation of the sound current may not make much sense. It takes experiencing the audible lifestream to comprehend what it is and why others class it as mesmerising and beautiful.

The vibration is the foundation of everything within our consciousness's perception; thus, every other sound has its base in the sound current. Any attempt to copy the sound current is bound to fail, as it has the sound current as a base. Compare it with a painter who creates a copy of a scenery in nature. A good artist can capture the scenery's feelings and mood, but it will be different when experiencing the real place. Experiencing the sound current is like this; it touches our whole being and soul, and it forces us to keep on listening to its mesmerising sound.

At the higher levels, it becomes more like light, while some describe it as soundless sound. We do not need to know more; we can achieve hearing it, and by this, we know it exists. I found no proof that our science has isolated the vibration to the extent that we can listen to it via tools available, but, to me, this will likely happen at some stage during scientific progress.

-oOo-

As science has not yet been able to detect the audible lifestream, we need to follow spiritual literature to determine why we hear a sound and what this entails. The sound current is the basis for the creation of life. The literature informs us that it emanates from the nameless and returns to the nameless. The best way to describe this will be to catch the story's essence in a drawing.

Consciousness

```
┌─────────────────────────┐
│      Audible            │
│      Life               │
│      Stream             │
└─────────────────────────┘
```

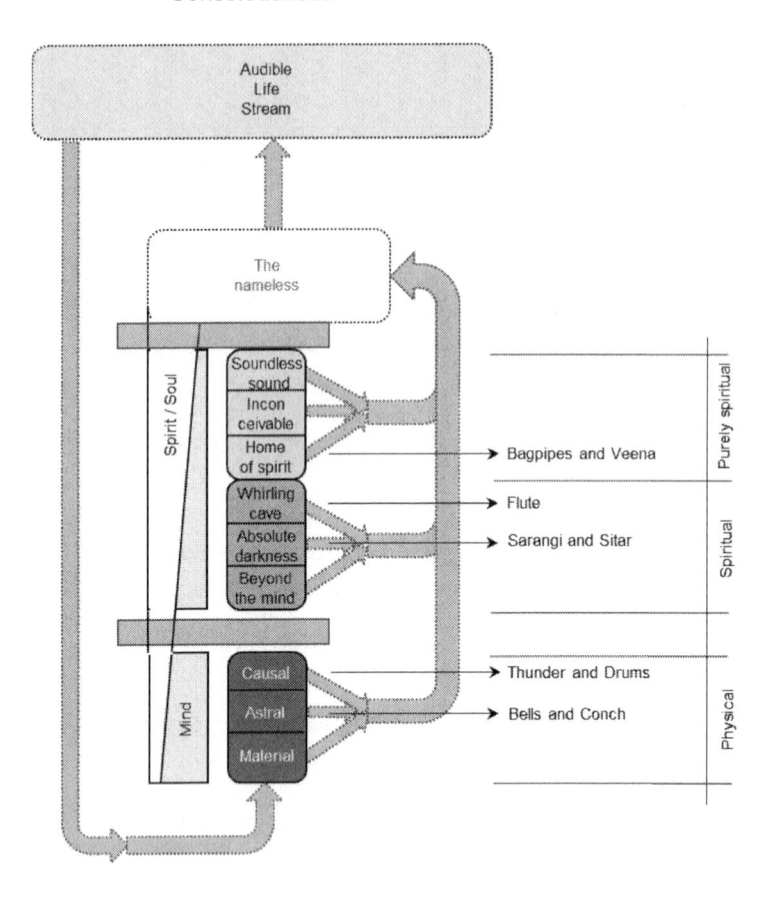

Spirit / Soul			
	Soundless sound		Purely spiritual
	Inconceivable		
	Home of spirit	→ Bagpipes and Veena	
	Whirling cave	→ Flute	Spiritual
	Absolute darkness	→ Sarangi and Sitar	
	Beyond the mind		

Mind			
	Causal	→ Thunder and Drums	Physical
	Astral	→ Bells and Conch	
	Material		

The audible lifestream emanates from the nameless. As the nameless is everywhere, we cannot catch it by an arrow, but to make it clear, I placed the nameless at the top of our consciousness, supplying the audible lifestream. From there, it goes down to all components in the universe. Everything that we can conceivably detect is part of the audible lifestream; consequently, this sound will be a combination of all frequencies in existence. We can hear this as a buzz.

When something gets created, it becomes more detailed. It assumes a particular frequency to become a specific item. The result is that such a thing emanates a specific frequency, which it distils out of the infinite amount of frequencies available. When we tune in to one particular domain of our consciousness via the process of meditation, we can hear the set of frequencies allocated to this area.

The people who managed to access the various areas of our consciousness via meditation compared their experience of these domains with musical instruments. These particular sounds are in the drawing. The realm beyond the mind has no allocated sound. The area is a pass over; when we arrive there, we go quickly to the wirling cave, and we will not be waiting to allocate the related sound. It will be there, but we do not want to stay long enough to hear the melody. The area of absolute darkness has a sound. For most people, this area is frightening, as we need to learn to use our feelings to sense our surroundings. At the Material level of awareness, the sound is a buzz, and when people listen to it, they do not know whether it is tinnitus or the audible lifestream. The two highest areas do not have sound allocated. At this level, we experience the frequency as something else, which some refer to as beautiful light.

The whole explanation indicates that at each level, somehow, we can understand what goes on and comprehend sufficiently to convert the experience into words and a drawing that we can understand at the material level of awareness. We can only achieve this when the mind is still influential in some way. As long as we can describe and talk about "we", the mind must have some influence.

From the type of sounds, we can deduce that the higher we focus our attention on our consciousness, the higher the sound's frequency. What happens is that at the lowest level, we experience all the frequencies. The higher we climb in our consciousness, the lower frequencies filter out, and the sound leftover is a combination of what is left over, i.e. a high tone. When we arrive at the purely spiritual level, the remaining frequencies are so high that they are not in the realm of what we refer to as sound; it becomes a form of light. We also note that all frequencies return to the source; the whole system is a circulation of an infinite amount of frequencies. In spiritual literature, we find that locating the audible lifestream source is not possible; it is everywhere. As the nameless is everywhere, the audible lifestream emanates from everywhere. We can, therefore, not pinpoint a point of origin.

Everything that exists requires two components: The static energy and the audible lifestream. This combination becomes the creation. The description of a Trinity, the energy, the audible lifestream, and the creation, we can find in many reference books and religions. Behind the Trinity, we see the nameless. When people discuss God, they refer to this concept, the creator of all.

-o0o-

The audible lifestream has in spiritual terms a particular use. It allows those on the path to counter the vices of desire and attachment, both powerful chains that hold the soul to the material level of awareness. Desire is a powerful force. It keeps our attention occupied until we pass away, and it never gives up. Even when we lay on our death bed, desire is still prevalent; we wish to continue living. Desire always leads to the wish for ownership; we want to buy or acquire what we desire. The combination leads to attachment; we do not want to part with the object of our desire.

By learning to become mesmerised by the sound current, we counter the material forms of desire. However, the earthly desires are so strong that even highly developed spiritual people can fall back to their attraction.

-o0o-

This brings us to the concept of our attention. We use the term a lot, but what does it entail in spiritual terms?

People use attention to focus on a subject. Ordinary people do not receive specific training to control this focus, and their concentration strays continuously. From a young age onward, some of us can focus attention precisely, and these people become very good at a specific subject. Often, they also are good at related matters, as they instinctively know how to concentrate. The art of such concentrating attention is a requirement when we learn to meditate.

When we ask people to concentrate their attention on the third eye centre, mostly, they can hold this focus for a few seconds only. To progress on the spiritual path, we must keep our attention on this spot longer, preferably continuously. When we learn to focus and concentrate our attention, the span narrows.

Compare this with a flashlight. To make the beam intense, manufacturers insert a focal lens in the lamp to make the light beam smaller but more directed. We should learn to do this with our attention. The focus will let us hear the audible lifestream vibration of the next level after our material awareness level, the astral level. When we hear this, it sounds like a bell or a conch. It is a deep melodious sound built up from various frequencies.

After maintaining our focus longer, the sound becomes different, like thunder or drums. Both these sounds are a combination of a lot of frequencies. Our concentration is still on the outer path, at the physical level of awareness; therefore, most of what we experience relates to the created matter.

To move to the spirit level, we need to jump from the part of our consciousness governed by the mind. The awareness level we now enter is entirely new to us; nothing we have ever experienced can compare.

The mind created the dimension of time, and via this invention also made the other dimensions happen. Therefore, the concept of space disappears, concepts like infinity, vibration, and measurements are gone. We do not have the use or the senses as we experience these at the physical levels of awareness. Although some of the mind's influence is still apparent, we arrive at something that we can only describe as "Nothing".

This part of our consciousness is frightening for anybody who only knows the physical levels of awareness, and we need somebody to assist us in getting through this phase. Those who did this did not describe a sound for this area. We need to move past this domain to arrive at the territories where we can learn what the spirit area means, and when we manage to concentrate our attention on the spiritual level and the purely spiritual level, we will feel at ease. The effect of the vibration of the audible lifestream in these domains is fantastic, and those that know from experience are forever different.

When we reach the higher levels of our consciousness, the final experience is that we consciously know that all we experience is one. There are no numerous personalities in this universe; we are all one.

The amount of information created by now is sufficient to proceed on the path to total awareness of our consciousness. We may see this as the final goal of our efforts, but it is not. The vision we have is to return with our soul to the vast ocean of the nameless.

To summarise this chapter: When we manage to concentrate sufficiently on the third eye centre to experience the audible lifestream, we will, eventually, experience the whole of our consciousness.

-o0o-

Proceeding on the Path

In my book, The Alternative, I describe the traditional direction that we should follow to gain awareness of our consciousness and, eventually, the nameless. The path involves a complete change of lifestyle for Western people, We change our diet, and we sit for daily meditation exercises. Following these rules, we may, at some stage, receive initiation. From that point on, we move our way up through the various domains of our consciousness.

I am a firm believer in the path of the masters, but as an engineer, I identified a few inconsistencies. Let us define these:

> Following a path involves the dimension of time. How is this possible when time is only apparent at the physical level of our consciousness?

> No time means that there are no distances. Everything occurs in the same place. Even the term "place" is not relevant when time is not a factor. Why the need to follow a path?

> The nameless is everywhere. Again, why do we follow a path to get to what is here?

Although most spiritual literature describes what we go through as a path, based on these considerations, I prefer to refer to following a process of increasing our awareness. A drawing I used in another book can make this clear:

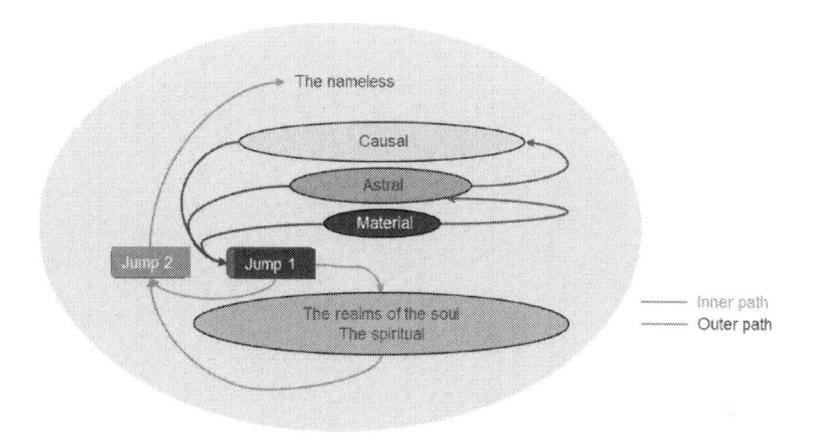

In this drawing, we indicate the outer path and the inner path as the traditional way to gain awareness of our consciousness's totality. However, as the nameless is everywhere, we, in theory, could straight step to the nameless. We do have to make the two jumps, of course. Such an approach would allow us to gain an understanding of all parts of our consciousness straight away; no need to go through all the hassle of meditating for years to develop a new way of living and thinking. Why can we not follow this clear and simple direction to our goal?

The answer is: We can.

As always, there is a "but" to such simple answers. As long as we have an attachment to the lower levels of our consciousness, we refuse to enter the domain of the nameless, as this means that we forfeit our ego. The literature tells us that karma stops progress on the path. We can show this in a drawing as well:

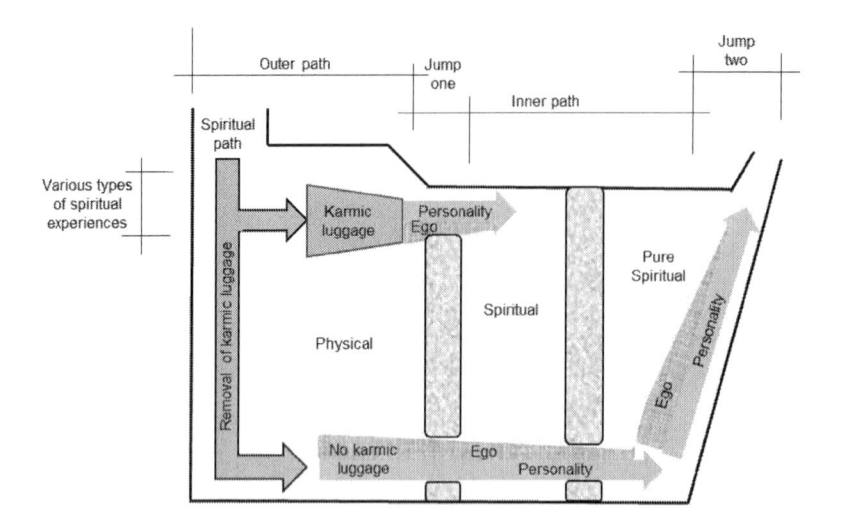

The drawing shows the passages which may allow a personality to progress, provided that its size fits through. The reality is that the indicated karma luggage and ego, which block progress, are self-inflicted. Let us discuss the drawing in detail.

At an early point during our development, we could move through the shortcut to the spiritual level. As the opening is there, we will get some spiritual experiences, but these are short and spaced out. However, these glimpses give us some idea of why we work to progress, motivating us to continue. We still have all our attachments to the physical world; thus, we cannot fit through the passage.

I call it luggage, as this term means that we could, if desired, shed this unwanted material and continue. The unfortunate reality is that we do not want to shed our dear possessions and attachments. We love to play little power games with those around us. We enjoy getting angry about the unfairness we experience. We love to show how good and essential we are by accumulating money and assets. Having excellent meals out, drinking a bit too much alcohol, even driving around in the countryside with our car is part of the attachments that stop us from progressing on the spiritual path.

We also do a lot of good things for the world, and we feel good about doing this; we feed our ego with the knowledge of the good we do. All these activities create luggage that ties us to the physical level of awareness. We can have a glimpse at the level of the spirit, but when we are not ready to let go, there is nothing in this world that can persuade us to shed our luggage. We need to go through a cleaning process before we can attempt to follow the path. We do not have to satisfy others; we, and nobody else, needs to be ready.

-o0o-

My explanation indicates that it is solely a system that involves our decisions at the material level of awareness. To be correct, it applies to all levels of awareness below our present level. We are not stopped by angels and by God; we do not progress based on ourselves. We receive the stories of demons that stop us because people always look for ways to blame others. Those who taught us know this issue, and to avoid losing followers, they included ordinary thinking in their teachings. The human mind's development is a process, and we should not start the teachings with the whole truth. Such a process our mentors use during school and university education, and the masters use it for spiritual teachings.

-oOo-

After shedding the luggage, which generally we refer to as compensating our karma, we can pass to the domain of the spirit. What we now see is that we still carry the ego; we are aware of ourselves. We find this explanation in the previous chapters. At the spiritual level of awareness, we also recognise personalities. The last bit of luggage we need to get rid of is this feature. Only then are we ready to merge in the ocean of all that exists. The drawing indicates all these requirements as small passages through which we cannot pass. Of course, this is a simplification of reality. We can always pass, but we do not want to shed the attachments that stop us from passing.

Compare it with learning to swim. We love to go to the deep end, where we see our friends playing water polo. To do this, we need to learn the basics of swimming and standing in deep water, else going that way gets us in dire straits.

-oOo-

At all times, we can continue all the way to the nameless and merge in the ocean of all. The various controls that the mind exercises to slow us down can easily help us move quicker. However, we need to be completely ready.

Being prepared to go all the way to the nameless does not mean that we meditation most of the day and behave as we get told to do by spiritual literature or physically by a master. Being ready means that we enjoy the physical world and all its pleasures, but we have no wish to stay at this level of awareness. We had enough; we prefer to return to our ultimate destination.

-oOo-

The universe is a complex unit of vibrating energy that moves in time. At the various levels of awareness in the physical, there are many worlds, each with personalities. Spiritual stories show that these entities are like humans. Those who explore the astral world compare the entities they meet with a human, but it is doubtful that such entities have a human shape and form.

At the material awareness level, we look everywhere in the universe for alien life forms, as we do not like the idea that we are alone in this vast universe. We do not comprehend that we are not alone; everything around us is in some way alive. This statement does not apply only to our world; it applies to the complete universe. If anything we observe were not alive, it would not be there. The differences we observe between the various objects relate to the amount of awareness they possess. Scientists in India even proved that a simple stone has a form of awareness. The concept of death as we experience this means matter with very little awareness. Even this definition is in some way flawed; we do not know for sure how much awareness we may find in, e.g. a rock formation. We cannot measure this, and our capabilities of feeling what goes on are severely limited.

When we pass away, the astral body leaves the material body. The body loses its awareness, and slowly, it returns to dust. I say slowly, but in the context of the universe, it goes to dust very quickly. Keeping our material body in existence, e.g. by embalming, is, therefore, not a good plan. It means that some of our awareness stays behind, while we may prefer it all to go with the rest. The Eastern way of burning the body may be more appropriate. We do not know for sure if this is a correct statement but give it a thought. We need to get rid of attachment to the physical domains; why keep part it going?

The astral body longs for a return to the material awareness level, and it selects a body to be born again. I now firmly believe that it is the attachment to the material awareness level that causes a rebirth. There are no black angels who punish us for bad behaviour and force us back to earth to sort out our residual karma. Everything that happens to us is the result of our wishes and beliefs. We build up a lot of attachments during our life, and these act like chains, tying us to the material awareness level. In other words, we love this world, and we do not want to leave.

-o0o-

When we receive initiation, we will not phase the black angels; our master guides us to do what needs doing to reduce residual karma and brings us to higher awareness levels.

Here we note again that we follow outside interference. The master is, in reality, the inner guide, which is our self from the higher levels of our consciousness. Spiritual writings, and those that received initiation, make us believe that initiation is a privilege, without which we cannot move to the higher awareness levels. I follow this theory, but I do not think that only those who receive initiation will progress. When I would give in to this belief, I return to believing in religion and the system that entering heaven is only for members of a specific faith. Keep this in mind when reading this; everybody can move to higher awareness levels. The wish to achieve this, plus the effort put in, cause us to reach our goal. Some systems assist us, but compare this with education at a specific university; it is an excellent way to achieve knowledge, but it is not the only way. There are lots of different ways to receive an education.

Although I appear to deviate enormously from traditional spiritual thinking, I only translate terms like karma into energy. The rest of my thinking follows the concept of the single image that we call our consciousness. Regarding life as a control system is what I deduct from traditional teachings. My engineering mindset looks at how everything in nature works together, and I apply this to our development. All I do is use a Western perspective to Eastern belief systems.

-oOo-

I want to touch on how to proceed on the spiritual path when we know that we need assistance from a person who is aware of the consciousness regions. The spiritual belief is that we cannot find a person like this; such a person is exceedingly rare, and we cannot distinguish this person from ordinary people. He or she hides in plain view. We need to analyse what this means and how to interpret such a statement, rather than sitting back in utter disillusion, knowing that out of billions of people, there are only a handful of people in the world who can assist us. How can they ever find us?

The way to sort this issue is to keep on living and enjoy life. When we are a seeker, we execute meditation and do our utmost to hold to the dietary requirements for a disciple. When the time is right, something will happen to us. Events happen to us all the time during our lifetime, and we must recognise such events. We should never assume that we are ready, and we are not fortunate as no master turns up.

Regarding ourselves prepared is a form of attachment. We need to be free from the first four vices as much as possible. When that happens, somebody will turn up who can assist. We should accept all assistance we receive; do not reject something because we feel that the person we meet is not qualified. The concept of qualification is a material awareness level term; another attachment. Leading a happy life and accepting what happens unconditionally is the best preparation we can execute before getting anywhere near to continue appropriately on the spiritual path. Even asking, "why do we want this direction?" is already a form of attachment that holds us back.

Various masters told us numerous stories of beggars and low-level craftsmen, who proved to be spiritual sages. These stories got conveyed for a reason; we need to listen and accept what they meant to tell us. When we are ready, we know who we need, and the people we require to assist us are usually not highly qualified in earthly terms.

-o0o-

Life is not what we want it to be. We tend to require a purpose, but that expression belongs at the material awareness level. So does thinking. When we do not use our mind as much, the concepts of thinking and duality disappear.

Lastly, we lose being a personality. We finally become part of "Nothing". Within this Nothing, we retain all the knowledge ever conceived, but as we give up our awareness, this is of no use. How can we ever grasp such a concept at the lowest level of understanding? As we become aware of the nameless, we have everything we can ever wish for, we know all there is to know, and we do not do anything with these assets. Even considering such things as assets is not correct; in the totality of what happens, an asset has no meaning.

-o0o-

The behaviour of an Initiate

When we commence on the path, we need to follow the rules set by the master who executes the initiation. These rules apply solely to the behaviour at the material level of awareness. When I analyse the process that leads to spiritual initiation, it gives me the impression that the process is mainly symbolic. I do not implicate that this process is not necessary or that we do not have to adhere to it; in my view, it is an essential step on the path of spiritual development. The various requirements have a meaning; the intention is to change our mindset and our body.

Each person follows his or her unique spiritual development path. At some stage, we need to comprehend that part of this development is to learn to listen to the inner voice we all possess. The inner voice, or the inner master, does not communicate via the use of a language. The concept of a language exists only at the material level of awareness. The development of this communication tool and all related to it, like speech and writing, is specific for humanity only. Our inner voice communicates to us using feelings.

The initiation process assists us in understanding this communication method. In previous chapters, I discussed the concept of personalities. The inner voice that we discuss here is a personality at the astral level who can help us follow the path. When the master who executes the initiation has an awareness of all levels of our consciousness, the connection at the astral level allows us to jump to the spirit level and continue our aim to become aware of all levels.

This chapter does not describe the actual process of initiation. The method of initiation is personal between the master and the disciple.

Why do we need initiation?

The world knows various spiritual development systems. Each of these systems recognises in some form the concept of initiation. Some systems use the initiation system as purely symbolic; baptism is an excellent example of such a system. Other systems follow a stepwise approach, while in yet more systems, it is a once-off step in our development.

When we study lifeforms at the material level of awareness, it appears that life attaches itself to a material body. We recognise two main entities; the material body and life itself. When life settles in a body, we call life, at times, the soul of the body. A well-known way to explain the concept of life is to compare life with an ocean. Every individual life form constitutes a drop in this ocean. To analyse life, I will follow this example. Be aware that this analysis is a simplification; the reality is a lot more complicated.

A large ocean will have on the surface a lot of movement. The deeper we go to the bottom, the more the ocean becomes a single water mass with little movement. At the very bottom of the ocean, the water is still. The surface contains various contaminants, like air bubbles, etc. The surface is not all water.

Assume ourselves to be a drop in this ocean.

To explore the bottom, we need to become identical in weight and consistency to the water at the bottom of the ocean. We need cleansing to become like the water at the bottom. The cleansing process we refer to as the dietary requirements and the changes in our behaviour. After the cleansing process, we can move down in the ocean. We mix with the rest of the water and offload everything that keeps us at the surface. We call this offloading process of contaminants paying off karma. We also have to recognise that we are one with the ocean. We are not an individual drop of water. By becoming one with the water in the ocean, we know the ocean's bottom and understand its surface. We know that we are one ocean; we are the ocean.

All life contains the path to achieve this level of understanding. To find the path to complete comprehension, we need a guide who can show the way. We all carry this guide inside of us; some refer to this guide as the inner master. The initiation process intends to connect those that linger at the material awareness level – the ocean's surface – to this inner guide. Finding this inner guide, or inner master, without assistance is possible. As is the case with all learning, it is easier to find the path when we receive assistance.

Symbolic Background

I studied the process that leads to initiation and the reason for initiation. What I have not much encountered is the symbolic meaning of the process. As this is essential to the process, those seeking initiation should be fully aware of the symbolism. Specifically, we should avoid that we do not get tempted to follow the path of judging others.

Most ordinary people follow the path of judging others. We continuously compare others with ourselves, and this comparing process indicates that we do not realise that each of us is on a unique spiritual path.

Why do I single judging others as something to avoid?

The process of judging contains several phases that relate to jealousy, greed and attachment. The way people communicate and look at others have many aspects of this way of thinking. As it is hard to distance ourselves from this issue, the best thing to do is be consciously aware. We cannot stop judging easily, but we can be mindful of our actions.

-oOo-

Before initiation takes place, we go through a cleansing process. We clean our body by holding for a minimum of six months to the following diet:

- Completely vegetarian - no animal meat at all
- No eggs
- No smoking
- No alcohol
- No recreational drugs

We need to understand each of these steps' symbolic meaning, as it is not the body that requires cleansing; the changes required happen to our mindset.

Vegetarian

As a potential initiate on the spiritual path, we need to appreciate the value of life. To show that we understand this requirement, we do not consume any animal flesh. The background is that when we kill anything, we create negative karma.

To continue living in the material world, we must always consume something that has been, or is at present, alive. To reduce creating negative karma as much as possible, we only consume the lowest life form, reducing negative karma production to a minimum. Eating meat – especially red meat – causes increased aggression in animals and people, reducing our ability to concentrate. Aggression and lack of concentration make meditation less effective; thus, avoiding the consumption of meat enhances the process of meditation, which is a much more important reason for becoming a vegetarian.

Masters noticed that the concentration capability of humans when killing other life forms decreases. Depending on the level of awareness in these life forms, the reduction of humans' concentration capability varies, and the period for the decline in concentration changes. Based on this knowledge, the masters produced a ranking system:

    1 - Humans
    2 - Mammals
    3 - Birds
    4 - Insects
    5 - Plants

The concept of ranking is typically a human reaction, and funny enough, humans are on top. Furthermore, a ranking process is a form of judgement, and potential initiates should refrain from judging. Another issue is that a carnivore can never develop spiritually.

Although I have a lot of respect for those that taught us spiritual lessons, I do not believe that life works in this way. I do not profess to know more than the masters, but I know that the masters adjust their teachings to what their disciples can comprehend to ensure that people follow their advice. I, therefore, follow a slightly different belief. All life develops spiritually. Although humans regard themselves as the highest life form, the reality is probably different.

Humanity is on an evolutionary path, and a step we took in the past was to leave living largely sub-consciously at the material awareness level – we left paradise. We now must become fully aware of the material awareness level, but we must also learn to consciously follow our inner voice guidance.

Symbolically, the vegetarian lifestyle is excellent for a human. Within the window of possibilities at the material level of awareness, we show the intention to be clean, as clean as we can get. However, we can never be completely clean, as we must eat to keep on living, and we can only eat something that is or has been alive.

Some people assume that they can avoid killing other life forms completely. These people forget that our digestive system contains many micro-organisms, and we kill bugs and micro-organisms continuously. We must be realistic; we kill, always. Therefore, we should be very humble, as we are aware of the issue that we must kill to survive. We cannot blame people who are not aware of the issue for their lifestyle. As seekers, we are aware; we know that we can never be completely clean.

From this analysis, it also follows that we should never look down on others who live their lives differently. Others follow their unique path in life. Their path is not our path.

Symbolically, this is the message of the vegetarian lifestyle:

> We live our lives very humble.
>
> We direct sufficient attention to meditation.
>
> We do not direct too much attention towards following the food requirements, as we can never achieve the objectives of these requirements for 100%.
>
> We should not assume that only humans can develop spiritually.

No eggs

An egg is the symbol of life before it commences its journey at the material awareness level.

To show our respect for life, we should not destroy the basis of life. We show our respect for life by not eating eggs. We also know that the masters found that our concentration capability, which we require for proper meditation, reduces when we consume eggs. Of course, we will be eating nuts, apples, etc. These items are the basis for the life of plants.

Here again, we shall be humbled; we are aware that we can never be completely clean. The symbolic gesture of refraining from eating eggs will also teach us to not look down on others. We follow our path, and we have the intention to show respect for life. However, we must also live. We are aware that we cannot hold to the requirement altogether.

Not eating eggs is a symbolic gesture. We should not contaminate this gesture by looking down on others. Looking down on others is judging.

No smoking, no alcohol, no recreational drugs

Our body is the house of our soul. Being aware of this, we need to ensure that our body stays in excellent condition. We, therefore, should not contaminate our body with anything that is not clean.

Drugs cause the mind to become less suitable for proper meditation. The potential initiate should, therefore, avoid drugs to allow the body to be in excellent condition. Unfortunately, the material world contains various contaminants in the air we breathe and the food we consume. We are aware of the requirement and the reasoning behind the condition, but we are also mindful that we can never wholly adhere to the situation.

Our intention is correct, but the reality of the material world causes issues. We should, therefore, be very humble. We know that we cannot be what we intend to be. When we are not aware, we cannot help this, but being conscious means that we know that we are not clean. As said before, we do not look down on others who use these drugs; we are not totally clean either. We become humble and avoid judging.

-oOo-

The potential initiate must realise the symbolic importance of the requirements for initiation and the impossibility of completely adhering to these requirements. It is the symbolism of the preparation for initiation that is the most critical part of the process, and that the potential initiate intends to understand the reason for the requirements and adhere – as much as is realistic – to these requirements. The objective of this preparation is to clean ourselves of thoughts that are not suitable. Eventually, this leaves us with only the thoughts of love and devotion.

Any judging of others – being humans, animals or plants – pulls us back to the circus of life and play our role on the stage. We noticed that in all the preceding, we warned for the factor judging. It is one of the most common things that affect progress on the spiritual path, and it is also something that all people do very frequently.

-oOo-

People who live their lives mainly in a subconscious way are in the process of getting to the awareness phase. They require our assistance; we should not treat these people as lesser beings. The concept of "lesser" is part of a judgemental process. When we judge anything, we will be living at the lowest level of awareness, and we do not progress on the spiritual path.

The Path to Initiation

We do not hold to the requirements before we receive initiation; we live the requirements.

What is meant by this statement is that we understand the background for each of the requirements. We do not stop after we receive initiation; we live this life, as we firmly believe in this way of living. We learn to love everything alive because we have been there at some stage during our spiritual development.

The initial period

Not eating meat is not easy. Most of us at some stage in our life ate meat, and when we shop for food, the supermarket is filled up with products that we should not eat or drink. We join friends for a night out. They start with a good meal in a restaurant. With the meal comes a bottle of wine, and of course, before starting, they have an alcoholic beverage. Why is this process so bad?

Enjoying life is not bad. During our life, we encounter situations that challenge our body. We learn to recognise these situations and what is proper and healthy. In animal life, young animals learn from their parents and the rest of the group to which they belong. The situation with humans should be similar, but it is not.

When we look at food alone, what we learn is what is tasty. That is not the same as what is healthy. We learn to overeat. We learn to drink alcohol, use drugs, we smoke. Although the people in the world become more aware of what they eat, the primary knowledge about food is still its taste, not what nourishes the body. The use of any form of drugs is part of most habitual behaviour amongst people. In such a cultural environment, we cannot expect a human being to develop a sense of what would be suitable for the body.

The process towards initiation contains a challenging test for the Western potential initiate. We must learn to adjust our way of living and embrace a much more Eastern food culture. In the process, we set ourselves apart from those that are part of our group. It is the process of perseverance and discipline that we must embrace, plus the continuation of mixing with our friends. Our path is not their path. We adhere to the requirements, but we should also enjoy watching our beloved friends enjoy themselves. At some stage in their life, they will go through a phase like us.

> Now, how do we deal with the habit of meeting others for an alcoholic drink?

> What about going for a social visit to the pub, meeting friends?

> Do we buy food for those we look after and is this bad?

> Even worse, do we force those we love to live like us?

We do not force a change on others, and we do not judge others. It is our personality that we attempt to adjust. We can join in with people who drink alcohol, while at the same time we drink non-alcoholic drinks. Statements that we do not want to mix with people who drink alcohol and eat meat have their basis in judging these people.

We will not be a proper potential initiate when we do not remove judging others from our way of behaving. When we distance ourselves from the realities of the world, we act like a hermit. The creation of the world meant to allow learning; we do not distance ourselves from the world because we have the perception that the world is wrong. When people behave like we would not behave ourselves, let them be, and remember that we did things that are not part of our present behaviour pattern. Others are never wrong; the absolute wrong is when we judge others who do not do what we do.

Later on

We can test ourselves to know whether we are ready for initiation.

The way other people live their lives will not be an issue for the person prepared for initiation. Mixing with others, even when they eat and drink different from us, is not an issue. We can joke and laugh and stay light about a habit we have. We assist others who would like to be like us, but we also are willing to help those who are not following our path without changing their way to our approach.

When we eat vegetarian, we need to study what this means for our body. Our everyday food contains all sorts of vitamins and proteins which our body requires. We need proteins, carbohydrates and fat, plus various minerals. Removing eggs and meat from our diet requires knowledge about replacing the nutrients which originate from these parts of our food. Eat lots of nuts and lentils and enough fruits each day. Never assume that we can live at the material level of awareness without killing anything.

When not killing becomes the focus of our life, we misdirect our attention. The focus of our attention must be on the third eye centre. The food adjustment is mainly symbolic, and when we understand why, we will happily embrace the requirements without going over the top. Daily meditation is our priority.

> The way of life we should embrace is to be happy.
>
> When we judge others, we cannot be happy.
>
> When we are not happy, we cannot meditate with love and devotion.
>
> Keep in mind this sequence of behaviour.

-oOo-

The Physical

The physical level of awareness is everything that falls under the total control of the mind, and the dimension of time is part of this governance. Most people on the path never go beyond this vast awareness area of our consciousness.

-o0o-

We all know our world very well. We live here, and it is familiar. Our scientists study whatever happens, and their knowledge increases continuously, at a vast pace. However, I got a few questions to answer:

Do we know where we live?

Who constructed all the elements available on this planet?

Is what we experience real?

What does this word "here" entail?

The previous part of this book showed a different way to look at our world. We can add some more in this chapter. A substance we are familiar with, matter, which we experience always, is an illusion. We know that it consists of particles, which themselves are energy in vibration. If we could experience matter precisely as we find it around us, we would see a seemingly empty area, with vibrating energy at some places that appear to have some form of cohesion, as they form shapes. Although the distance between the vibrating parts is enormous, compared with the size of these particles, the cohesion is of such strength that the shapes are mostly constant. When we increase the temperature, the distance between these particles increases and the cohesion appears to become less intense.

Rather than describing what we may see and how we perceive the physical with perfect sensory organs, let us analyse this world and its inhabitants. I will use a tool to clarify the story in the format of a drawing. As a basis for the explanation, I use spiritual knowledge.

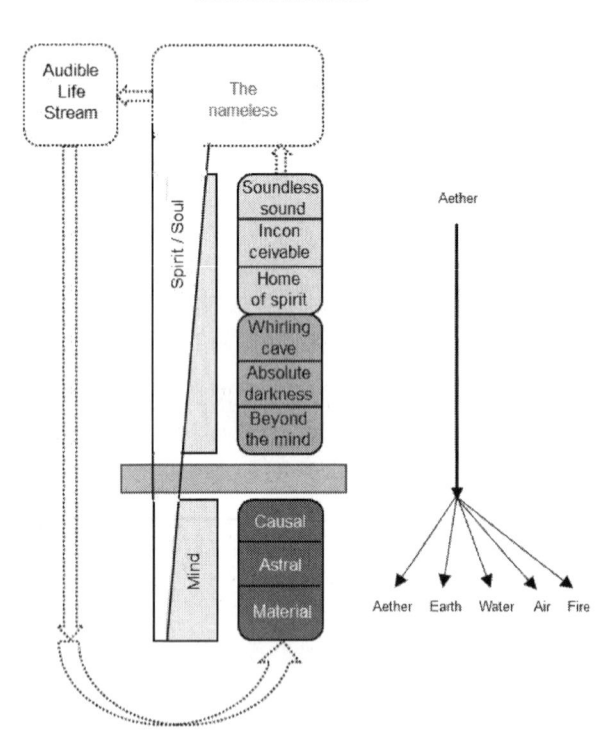

The drawing of consciousness I provide here we discussed in previous chapters. The masters from the past explained that we recognise a substance referred to as aether at the domain we call our home at the spiritual level. This substance spreads out into earth, water, air, fire and aether at the material level. When I studied at technical college, this explanation got ridiculed by one of my teachers. He referred to it as a sign of progress; we know so much more these days. However, my teacher did not realise that the knowledge conveys a principle related to matter, not a chemical consistency.

All matter has four forms, solid (earth), fluid (water), gas (air) and plasma (fire). Science recently defined three more states, but these relate to the absolute zero temperature and temperatures higher than those of stars. Knowledge of the past looked at realistic possibilities in the universe. In the past, aether went through various descriptions, and science could never prove that it exists. However, scientists, presently and in the past, felt that an element like aether must exist; it is the composing element of celestial bodies.

It is not the intention to prove science wrong and refer back to old theories about matter. The old views cover the consistency of what exists outside the domain of matter, and these theories took into account the higher levels of our consciousness. It does not matter to what level of consciousness we manage to focus our attention. We eventually will find that everything we experience is but an illusion.

-o0o-

The material level of awareness is a rough illusion. We find that we get lured to items we like, but the attraction is mostly not related to the experience. Why do we buy things while we do not need them? It gives us a good feeling. When we analyse this habit, we detect a drive to obtain something somewhere inside us. We get the item (read buy), and this satisfies the feeling. We walk around a shop and wonder what to buy next. We cannot have an essential use for items when we have to wonder what we need. Humans' habit of looking for things to possess led to advertising systems that tell people that they must buy something. We see it on TV, so we feel it would be a fantastic asset to add to our collection. We notice that celebrities have something, and if we can afford it, we want it.

The description of the buying culture of people applies to all habits we encounter at the material level. We want to own animals, so we buy them and put them in a cage. Nobody wonders whether the animal wishes for such treatment; anyhow, animals do not have feelings like humans is the standard way of thinking. We also argue that we treat the animal very well.

The same thinking applies to other people. We try to own others. Some systems used are relatively crude; people exercise raw power to make everybody around them do whatever they feel they want. Other methods are more subtle; careful manipulation causes others to become enslaved to such people. All these systems share one common factor; attachment. Both parties accept the roles they play, as they are attached to the material world.

As long as we are under complete control of the mind, these attachments will rule our lives.

What constitutes attraction?

To get to the bottom of this feeling, starting with an example seems the best approach.

We see a beautifully coloured bird, we like it, and we desire to own this animal. We go to a shop, buy a cage and the bird, and take it home. Within a few days, we get used to the bird's beauty, but we do not like cleaning the cage and buying food for the bird. The bird appears to have a mind of its own, another negative. Some people purchase such pets and release them back into the wild for these reasons. The feeling of attraction is not related to the reality of owning what we see. When we look at something, what we experience is not what we feel after obtaining the item.

What happens is that our mind continually creates this feeling of attraction to make us feel like we would feel when focusing our attention on the higher levels of our consciousness. The mind, in a way, loves to please our material body. However, the feelings are always short-lived and rather crude. We can spend a lot of money on a new car, which makes us feel fantastic, but only for a short time. After that, it is just another asset we acquired, standing in front of the house and costing money on insurance, maintenance and petrol.

From the examples, we deduct that the feeling of attraction does not relate to the habit of owning the item. What we do, is pleasing the eye and assume that it gives us something else. In some cases, we know what we expect; in other cases, we just obtain an item without even realising what we expect to feel. However, we hardly ever get what we expect when we give in to desire.

The best way to experience attractions is to go into nature and look at sceneries. Go to various places, and do not try to own such areas; just experience the appeal and beauty. The owning part is attachment, and it ties us with a chain like hold to the material awareness level.

Humanity also tries to copy the beauty created by the mind when we design something. As the feeling that the mind creates is already rather crude, the human design, which bases its look on what the mind made, will even be more elementary. Instead of improving our existence, we move more in the direction of the five vices.

Why do we continuously look for beauty?

We can see that attraction and beauty are, in some way, related. However, beauty is very different. Beauty is not associated with a physical occurrence; it is something we encounter when our senses have an outside experience. We recognise a relationship between the feeling and the outward experience, so we call something that causes the attraction beautiful. However, it is an experience that indicates a requirement for the body.

A stunning vista emanates energy, and those that experience the area feel more at rest. We love to sit down at such a place and soak in the beauty. People are aware of the effect, and sites like this attract many visitors, while particular spots even have seats installed. Loading up on energy makes us feel better. Our material body requires energy; it obtains it somehow from everything we consider beautiful.

Compare the story with what goes on with a flower. The flower is beautiful as it wants to attract insects. The colour and smell cause the initial attraction. The nectar inside the flower is something the insect learnt from being young onward. When the insect goes inside the flower to obtain the nectar, the plant pollinates the insect. The forgoing process guarantees the continuation of its kind.

We now touch on the requirement for the material body to top up with energy. As this appears to be a requirement, from where does the energy emanates? Mostly, we top up energy from eating and being out in the open air. When we feel good in a place, it means that we top-up on power.

We can also generate a top-up of energy by managing a crowd of people. After having such a gathering, people tend to say that they feel energised. As I indicated in previous chapters, energy is all around us, so we could top-up as and when required. However, this option appears closed to us; we need to follow the possibilities provided by nature.

Why is it that we fight for security?

All entities in the material world seem to wish to fight to obtain some form of security. They do this primarily to secure their existence, but humanity went a lot further; they fight to gain power. Obtaining influence over others constitutes the highest form of attachment; thus, humanity appears furthest removed from losing attachment. Does this mean that, contrary to our belief, humanity is the lowest life form in this world? Measuring levels is a typical human way of evaluating importance. Nature does not distinguish between life forms, they all received life at birth, and they all have to go through a mystical process during their lifetime and beyond. The statement that humanity is the most important form of life comes from humans. I do not believe that the spirit has a preference.

As I made this statement, do I contradict the masters of the past? I do not believe I do. Those masters had a task to educate their followers, and we cannot do this by telling them that they are the lowest life form in this world. It goes against most religions, and it may lead to the possibility of losing one's life. These days, people are different, and I believe that the present-day seeker can listen to what I say, understand it, and realise that the objective is to make us humble and not cause people to feel insulted.

Security is a requirement for all living entities to cause their species to continue living at the material awareness level. At the higher levels, it appears immaterial what goes on. As long as the concept of life is maintained, the system keeps on running.

Is duality something that exists everywhere?

Duality appears to be part of how the mind operates, similar to the dimension of time. As long as we follow the mind's leadership, we will not understand a world without duality. I can write about it in this book, but we must go beyond the mind's control to comprehend its meaning.

To a human, anything that states a condition must have an opposite. Good follows bad, small follow large, and so on. However, even in our physical way of thinking, some concepts do not have an opposite. Real love without attachment is such a thing. Happiness without a reason for being happy is another. Ideas like this do not belong at the material level of awareness; they are the poles that stick out from the spirit level to allow us to pull over the barrier. When we learn to realise this, we can cross the border to the spirit level with our inner guide's assistance.

-oOo-

At the astral level, we expect to see normal humans, but with radiant bodies, as that is what the spiritual literature tells us. The reality is that the entities that live at the astral level show their intelligence and awareness and their senses, albeit a lot more sensitive. We can find animals and entities that roamed the earth way before humanity came into existence. Any entity that manages to raise its awareness to this level will be there.

Some managed to raise their awareness higher, to the causal level. The mind resides at this level, and formally, the mind does not appear beyond its domain of control. However, based on stories, we must conclude that the mind has at least a sliver of influence all the way up to the highest level of the spirit. However, it is a minor influence; the mind is not in total control.

Some of those with an awareness of the highest level still have a body at the material level. It is this connection that causes the influence of the mind at the highest level. Not all the personalities that are part of the spirit level have a material body; most do not possess such a connection with the material awareness level. However, as long as one does, the mind's influence will be part of the personality. This interface between levels of awareness causes contamination by the mind of all levels of consciousness.

Why do I call this contamination? The mind's influence allows us to understand, up to an extent, the various domains at the level of the spirit. However, the concept of duality causes conflicts at the material level of awareness, and as long as it has some form of influence, conflicts will continue. Also, the concept of ego is a significant factor in the cause of conflict. Here again, we need to get free of these concepts before we are free from the bonds, or chains, that tie us to the world of illusions.

Before we free ourselves of everything we ever possessed, we first need to become free of our attachment to matter and desires.

-oOo-

Liberation from Matter

Now we get to a complex subject. We are matter, so how do we free ourselves from the substance of which we consist? Of course, we are more than matter. We also consist of aether, and somehow we are alive; our body contains a soul.

-o0o-

We need to address two issues at this point, which relate to liberation of matter;

> The feeling of desire
> The feeling of attachment

Desire relates to attachment and is a part of the draw by the mind that is difficult to get rid of, and it will not leave us, ever. Even when we focus our attention on the higher spiritual levels, we will always experience desire. In a broader sense, greed leads to attachment and the wish to own the item of our desire. We become like a slave of the mind, fighting, if required, to obtain and retain the things we love. When we do not appear to get these items, we create a feeling of anger or fear.

As these are items that belong at the material level of awareness, we cannot own any of them; they stay behind when we pass away. Although we mention physical items in this description, it applies to people and animals as well. It even applies to the way we look, the outward impression we love to create in the world of matter.

The only way to fight this strong force is to oppose it with a stronger desire, and that is the longing for the audible lifestream. No other system works permanently; using our character strength to discipline the mind may work for some time, but eventually, we will fall back. Even when we know how to listen to the sound current, we still feel the attraction of desire, the draw to own the subjects of our desire, and the related attachment to these subjects.

We may assume that we managed to rid ourselves of these feelings, but that is an illusion. As long as we own a material body, these feelings are part of our existence.

-o0o-

We now return to the concept of attraction but in the broader sense. Some people see what they class as a beautiful person, which relates entirely to the material level of awareness. They measure what constitutes beauty, which, in their view, goes with the dimensions of the body and the face. They hold beauty contests and muscled people contests. These are the people who adjust their bodies and faces because all they see is the attraction at the material level.

However, the real draw is at the higher levels of the physical. Those that experience the attraction without regarding the look they experience at the material level are in touch with the astral level. In a way, they have passed the material level of awareness, and they live at this higher level.

Some may now tell me that the literature suggests that the astral level is extraordinary, and my description does not appear to be consistent with this explanation. The issue is the same with buying a beautiful car; within a few days, we get used to its attraction, and we look for other ways to sense beauty. We need to realise that we need to look differently at people consciously. We do not see what others call handsome, attractive and beautiful anymore; we see something else, and this something else is the astral body. Those who see this will maintain this opinion when they get older, and they refer to their eighty-year-old partner as handsome and beautiful.

When we give this description a thought, we will realise that indeed for such a person, life is so much more illuminating than it is for those who only look at the material attraction. When we have the capability to look at people in this way, we passed the material level and liberated ourselves from matter. Not entirely, but to some extend.

-o0o-

However, this is only the first phase. I never aimed to describe progress at the spiritual level as easy; my description of the step to the astral level applied only to judging humans. We now need to use this to everything we experience at the material awareness level. We look at our house, and it is not the bricks and mortar we look at; we need to see the whole house. When we study a painting, we need to look at the whole of the picture, catch the feeling that the artist intended to convey and regard this impression as our way to judge the person who created the painting. When we walk in nature, we must look at the whole of nature and feel the energy that comes to us. When we can do all this, we live at the astral level and continuously top our energy levels.

What I describe is a lifestyle change, not a way to look at items in the world. We can keep on trying to look at the things we observe in the world and try to see the whole and feel the whole. By the end of our life, we will not be anywhere near to adjusting our opinion to everything, and we have not even started judging the universe. When we change our lifestyle and automatically see everything from a different perspective, we do not need to test ourselves to make sure we see the attraction in everything around us; we do it automatically. When we achieve this change, we live at the astral level.

The following step is to maintain the lifestyle we set ourselves. The spiritual literature talks about two different types of people; those who reach the astral level and those that are at all times living at the astral level. We know how difficult it can be to maintain a lifestyle, even when we sincerely try. Somebody sells us a car, and we establish that it was a con job. Do we see the beauty in the car and the salesman? Of course not, so we are back in the theatre of life at the material level. A very good looking person impresses us a lot, but when we find that our bank account is compromised and the person disappears, do we still regard the person as beautiful? Not likely. There is an essential point in these two examples. It is not the person who conned us; we looked at this person at the material level of awareness. When we continuously regard the world from the astral level, we would spot the person's issue.

Those living entirely at the material level do simple things to maintain their feeling of what constitutes enjoyment. Of course, the mind does this, but the pleasure created does not have to satisfy others living at this level of awareness. I do not want to go into the very dark type of examples, but a simple example is the previous con jobs. The people executing these feel happy. However, often they need to explain why they did nothing wrong. A statement like: "If people do not do their homework, they can expect to get in trouble, somebody does it, I can, just as well, be that somebody." Such a statement indicates that something inside this person tells them that what they did is not correct. We all get these messages, and often, we do our utmost to explain why what we did was acceptable. The deed is a typical crude way of the mind to create happiness at the material awareness level; the explanation shows that such a person still resides at this level.

We all can relate to this story, and we all can recall examples of such situations when we go back in our memory. Now we know that these are the moments that show us that we are connected to matter. Liberation from matter means that we stop these sort of activities.

-o0o-

The explanation appears fine, but it refers to activities created by the mind to give us pleasure. The mind uses the five vices to support these pleasures. As the mind controls the physical, how do we explain that these crude enjoyments disappear when we live at the astral and causal level? We cannot explain this because even when we manage to live continuously at higher physical levels, we still experience the mind's attractions. We can find examples in our history of experienced masters who fall back to these pleasures. It is up to the seeker to see these. When I mention those who fell back, it creates an apparent defensive mood in some people and a protective reaction in others. Writing this chapter aims not to cause division; the idea is to create an understanding of the physical levels of awareness and what we mean by the term "liberation from matter."

-o0o-

When we experience complete liberation from matter, we are there; no need to try to do more. Or, possibly, there is more to consider?

As long as the mind influences what we call our consciousness, we always feel the attractions generated, and we continuously need to fight off these enjoyments. The higher we manage to focus our attention on our consciousness, the more subtle the mind's actions. We think we can handle the crude and straightforward pleasures of the mind, and suddenly we find that we give in to something that seemed initially so utterly logical. We located another chain that tied us to either the physical or spiritual part of our consciousness. Total liberation from matter means, therefore, that we can divorce ourselves from the material level of awareness.

When we look back in history, we find those referred to as saints who managed to execute this feat. I will put a stop at this perception. Anyone who made it clear to the rest of the world how high they managed to reach sainthood did not achieve this; when it requires advertising, it means that they still have ties to the physical level of awareness. Some are to a lot of people exceptional. In some cases, they are unique, as they achieved, likely, a very high level of awareness, and they also managed to maintain this level of understanding. But as soon as this achievement requires to be made known to many people, we need to become sceptical.

The ties that bind us to the ego, and even the physical pleasures, are very subtle at the higher spiritual levels, but as long as we live in a material body, they will always be evident. We can try to deny these bonds, but that is not a sensible way to progress. To fight an enemy, we first need to identify this enemy and know its existence and location. Spiritual development works the same way. We cannot liberate ourselves entirely from anything, as long as we do not know or recognise that these chains exist. Compare it with animals living in a Zoo. When the Zoo creates an attractive and large scale environment, the animals may perceive that they live in the wild. To free themselves, they first need to recognise that their living condition is like a golden cage. Some even argue that their present habitat is a better life; they are safe in their prison. The statement may be correct, but the animals still live in a locked-up condition, and their freedom is conditional.

Humanity lives similarly. The material level of awareness is like a golden cage, which provides any living entity with many pleasures generated by the mind. However, it is an illusionary environment created by the mind. When we manage to enter the only reality that exists, it may not be perfect, and it may not be what we now perceive it to be. However, it is the reality; it is not an illusion. All literature describes the joining of the nameless concept as the most beautiful thing we ever can imagine. I find this description difficult. How can a drop of water feel happy when it joins the ocean. The ocean is possibly existing in a state of happiness, but the water drop will be gone; it merged in the ocean. It will take a lot of cleansing of our mind and bodily desires to get to a phase that we desire to disappear into "Nothing". Our destiny is to do precisely this, but it will take us time to create a way of thinking that allows us to accept moving this way.

-o0o-

Are there people we need to reach out to because, clearly, they must have reached the highest level of their consciousness?

Many people in our material world sell themselves as spiritual leaders, and in the process, they earn good money. These people created a business. Nothing wrong with having a business; it is what we do at the material level of awareness. However, it has little to do with spiritual development. We can follow courses with these people, subscribe to their websites, and visit their lectures. In some way, it assists us to develop, even if it only helps us to know the difference between what is real and what is an illusion.

The world will have people who are highly advanced on the spiritual path. These people will not speak about this with others. They know how far they still need to develop, and this knowledge makes them humble. They also are aware of the danger to fall for the pleasures generated by the mind. It gives an excellent feeling to attract many people who see somebody as something of a half God. However, it is another illusion, and it is not worth the risk of falling back to lower awareness levels.

The issues these people have are that they see it as their task to help others increase their awareness. How can one at the same time assist others and also ensure that they are not known for what they are?

To achieve such a challenge is the art of the real master. We only know how to do this when we reach this phase, but it will not be easy. If it were simple to achieve, every person in the whole world would become a master.

-o0o-

The Spiritual Region

The spiritual region is entirely alien to anything that we, as humans, ever experienced. The influence of time is minimal, as the mind has little effect in these regions. For clarity, I put the drawing of consciousness again in this chapter.

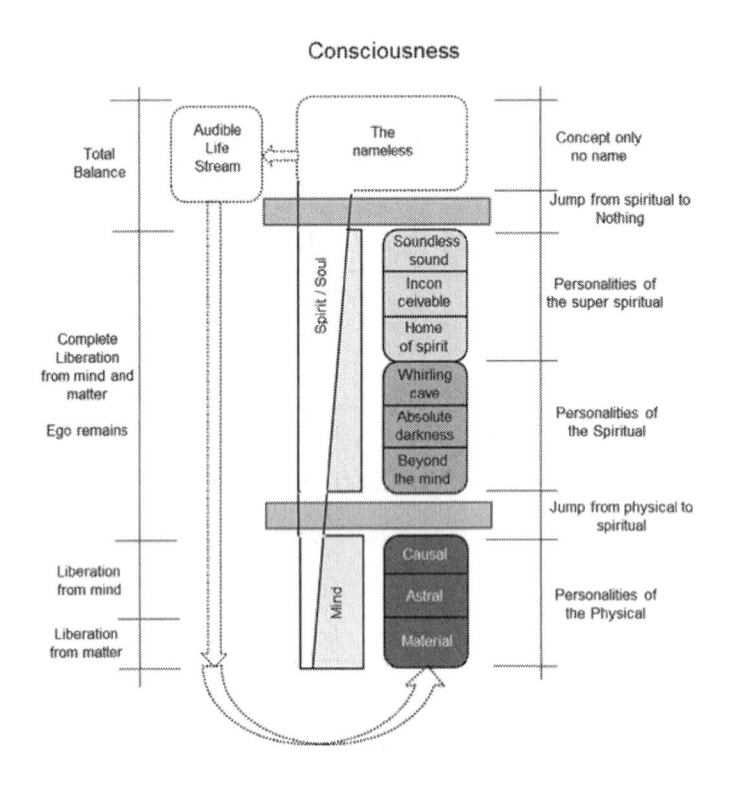

As soon as we move our attention to the spiritual regions, time and the other dimensions are not in existence. We feel the influence of these, as the material body is still part of us, and the mind has some impact. However, the experience is different. We experience everything of the physical levels of awareness from a distance; we are no longer part of these domains.

How to explain an area with no dimensions and with no concept of time? When we first become aware of the spiritual region, we initially experience only darkness. To understand this statement, we need to realise that we rely on our senses to create experiences. Therefore, our perception dictates that these must convey something. When this does not happen, logically, only darkness remains. Even the term darkness is not an accurate description; darkness is an experience we get when we are in an environment beyond our eyes' capability. It happens when the light in our place of existence becomes very dim.

The spiritual region we can only perceive directly, via our feelings and awareness. When we learn to use these facilities, the texture, initially, creates the perception of a wirling mass. I presume a baby straight after birth has similar experiences; until it learns how to use its senses, everything must feel like a wirling mass of experiences. When we get used to the experience and learn how to use our feelings and awareness, the area becomes comfortable; we are at the place we originate from; our home.

We need, again, to emphasise that we still have our material body. Of course, many of us assume that we are in deep meditation when we reach this region, and indeed, some of us will be in this state. However, the best way to explore our consciousness is to become aware of the totality when we are living our ordinary life. What is the use of an experience when we can only achieve it by sitting in a meditative state for prolonged periods? We need to eat, drink, work and enjoy ourselves. In general terms, we need to live and survive at the material level of our consciousness. We should not need to meditate to be aware of the totality of our body's components; thus, let us learn to create awareness of our consciousness during the period that we are awake. During the period we refer to as sleep, we have less control over our attention; it is better to start with the period that we have conscious control. I added a chapter on meditation to allow the reader to practise this skill.

When we manage to experience the spiritual region, and at the same time, execute, at the material level, our daily activities, the spiritual literature informs us that we achieved mastery. I agree that we are a complete human when we accomplish this capability; we are aware of all our components. Whether this justifies us being called a master is questionable. The term master belongs at the material level of our consciousness. Do we call a human with an awareness of all body components a master at this level? Every human is aware of the material parts of their body. It would mean that all humans are masters when viewed by those that can only access the material level of awareness.

When we experience all awareness levels, we are still seekers, but we are complete seekers; we know what we are. The Eastern term for people who reach this level of awareness is that they are perfect. The name does not relate to the ordinary meaning of perfect; it relates to the person being aware, always, of all awareness levels of consciousness. The initial reaction would be to ask: "Why do we call such people seekers?" The answer is that, although they are aware of the total complexity of the entity they refer to as consciousness, they still have a long way to go. Such people "seek" for those that require assistance on the path, and they "seek" for the direction they still have to go,

Even at the spiritual level, the influence of the mind is apparent via the material body. A person with this high level of awareness can fall back to the material level's pleasures. We can wonder what sort of person we encounter who has achieved a complete understanding of the spiritual level and falls back to the material level's enjoyments. As long as the mind has any influence, and the ego defines that we are a personality, we can always be compromised. Historic parables contain stories of Gods who return to the earth and mix with the ordinary people and enjoy the flesh's pleasures. These stories possibly, refer to the possibility of such a return to the material awareness level. In our present-day society, we do not appear to have people with the ability to reach these spiritual experiences; consequently, we do not know what such a return to the flesh entails.

-o0o-

Having made this statement that people with a high level of awareness do not exist in our society, is this correct? When a person reaches this spiritual level of awareness, such a person is exactly like any other ordinary person to the outside world. He or she possibly radiates a fantastic feeling that makes other people living in their vicinity feel calmer, a feeling that we can only describe as love, without any conditional attachments. However, most people would not recognise this feeling; they are too engrossed in their role in the theatre of life to feel anything that does not relate to their role. The person effectively hides in plain sight.

I met people who generate such feelings, and they are like ordinary people, but their presence is extra-ordinary. I never experienced a person with total awareness falling back to living at the material level of awareness. I, therefore, like to avoid guessing what sort of person this would be.

Spiritual literature informs us that the world always contains people who achieved total awareness. They are, in Sant Mat Yoga, referred to as Perfect Living Masters. The more I become aware of spirituality, the more I believe that these are the people who show us the way. Eventually, humanity must all go this way and become complete humans, in the sense that we are aware of our totality.

When we are lucky enough to reach, as a race, such perfection, the first thing we will likely realise is that this state does not only apply to humanity. We need to replace the term "humanity" with "living entity". Every living entity is part of what we call our consciousness. It is not our consciousness; it is a shared awareness of everything alive. We will also find that everything in our world is alive. All that we experience has some form of awareness, the bit we call our soul, the part that makes us a living entity. Another realisation will be that the whole of the universe is a living entity. We are back at personalities, and when we reach such perfection, we recognise the existence of these personalities and the fact that we are part of a number of these.

A human constitutes around 3.2 billion living entities we refer to as cells. The totality we refer to as I. Everything we experience is, in some way, part of one of the personalities in the universe and beyond. Everything we experience is part of a personality. Only when we go beyond the spiritual level will we encounter a concept that does not have a personality and does not have an ego. All that it has is awareness and intelligence. It constitutes the void that is everywhere, and at the same time, it is "Nothing", as we cannot detect it in any way.

This book refers to it as the nameless, but this is too simplistic a description. How can everything that exists emanate from "Nothing"? The audible lifestream stems from this void, and this emptiness makes all vibrations that create all that exists. The sound current leaves "Nothing", and it returns as multiple frequencies to "Nothing". The nameless is everything that exists, in perfect balance. No negative, no positive, only balance.

-oOo-

From this analysis, we move to what might be heaven and what is hell. Both these concepts are terms related to the material level of awareness. Even though every language has equivalent terms, they belong to the material world. We can accept everything that we experience at our material awareness level and live in harmony with life itself. When we achieve this, we live in heaven. We can also resist the life we lead as we desire another life. Such a person lives in hell.

When we manage to enter the higher levels of our consciousness, we start to experience our material life as a film we watch as a spectator. The art is to keep viewing the theatre of life as an audience and avoid playing a role. As soon as we enter the play, we also are subject to the laws that govern the earthly theatre. This includes the possibility to experience living in heaven or living in hell.

Of course, I now open myself to opinions of people who feel certain actions by what they regard as bad people need punishment. Other actions are so bad; they require severe punishment. We need to understand that people, by their actions, will execute punishment to themselves. The laws of the material level of awareness dictate that we need to defend ourselves, so this is the type of action we take. However, blaming others for their actions is not part of our to-do list. As soon as we judge or condemn, we play our role at the material awareness level. We get sucked into the theatre of life.

I am well aware of how difficult it is to follow this advice, but it is the only way to live our lives when we follow the spiritual way of thinking. Forget the concepts of heaven and hell; they are an illusion just as the rest of our experiences on the material plane.

By now, it should be clear that at every awareness level, we risk falling back to the material level of awareness, is there a possibility to avoid this altogether?

The reality is that the mind and the ego are part of the material body that we possess. The influence of these, especially desire, will follow us all the way, as long as we have a connection to the mind. We should not detest this or call the mind an evil instrument. Like everything that exists in our existence, the mind and its components have a purpose. We are not to question life's purpose; we live it, like all other living entities.

-o0o-

After the spiritual levels of awareness, we experience another void. This jump anybody can only make completely alone. No assistance is there; however, there is a path that we can follow. The audible lifestream is the only possibility. When we merge in the sound current, we will merge in what we call the nameless: no more personalities, no more influence of the mind, no more dimension of time. We disappear in what, to all intents and purposes, we should define as "Nothing". Even in Eastern descriptions, some indicate that this is the most frightening step to make. People shy away from this step. However, it is the step to the only reality that exists; thus, it cannot be frightening. As I mentioned before, to take any action in our progress, we need to be ready. To let go of our desires and ego is so tricky that it causes us to resist. Most people stop here, as the prospect of losing "I" is too daunting.

The best comparison to this phase I can find is the structure of light. When we mix all colours available, we end up with something we define at a scientific level as no colour; we created white light. The reality of white light is that we can re-create every colour in existence using a lens. The concept of the nameless works the same way. It is "Nothing", it cannot be detected, it has no personality, but the whole of the creation emanates from this "Nothing". When a person can permanently focus their attention on this level – which is not part of our consciousness – such a person is classed in Eastern terms as perfect but of a higher level.

The concepts of the nameless and the audible lifestream, together, create everything in existence.

To make the story more complicated, we need to admit that there is another entity behind the trinity of the creators and the created. I have not found out how to move to this reality. For now, it constitutes the backbone to all the created beings, a single existence responsible for it all.

-o0o-

Masters have disciples, and they steer those disciples to guide humanity. A lot of the tasks of a master can be executed by those that follow the master. Many people in the world mean well, but they are not masters in the sense of the description given in this book. These people tend to provide themselves with unusual titles to attract followers. They have attachments to the material world, and because of this, they love the attention they receive. However, they do assist people on the spiritual path. Until people are ready to proceed to the higher awareness levels of consciousness, such masters are suitable for them.

A master knows that people like this are beneficial to spread the concept of spirituality to those who are not ready to follow the higher levels of the path, but they need spiritual guidance. By guiding such low-level masters, these surrogate masters can assist others to continue their journey.

Real masters hide from ordinary people. They do not do this actively; until a seeker requires a master, they will not recognise such a person. Therefore, the spiritual statement is that a master hides in full view.

A master's task is to assist humanity in the background; they are not on TV, advertising their capability. They do not need to promote what they are; with their total awareness, the master will know who needs genuine assistance, and for these people, they arrange a meeting via the law of coincidence. However, often even people who need real help can receive this from lower-level masters.

As masters have a high awareness level, can they execute miracles?

Miracles are events that defy the law of nature. As a master wants to appear to the world as an ordinary person, why show tricks that defy this objective? At times, masters show their disciples some of their capabilities. They only do this when, in their view, such an event is a requirement.

Performing a miracle goes entirely against the goals that a master wants to achieve. Therefore, we will hardly ever see the performance of such events. To be more specific, a miracle shows attachment to the physical level. It pulls a master down to the awareness level of their followers. Any master is fully aware of the danger of showing off their capabilities. They actively will avoid tampering with the laws of nature.

What constitutes a master?

I answered this question above, but we find many people in the world who claim to be exceptional at the spiritual level and even call themselves master. What are these people?

An excellent way to earn a steady income is to sell spirituality to people who look for guidance. A seeker should realise what this means; it is a worldly business meant to generate revenue. I do not consider this wrong; there are many ways in the material world to create an income; this is one of them. However, it is not part of the path of spiritual development. Some of these people are excellent at generating stories that relate to spirituality. Following such persons is not wrong. We will eventually find that they do not give us what we need; thus, we look for another way to progress.

There is a limitation in our search for the right person to follow. As long as we search, we will not find anything. The reason for this apparent inconsistency is that we are programmed to look for earthly qualifications. We will not even look at a simple beggar, but when we locate a professor who teaches spirituality, we believe that we found what we need. Only when we let go of these perceptions will we discover the person who can assist us.

A person who has total awareness of all levels of consciousness is unlikely to be a high-ranking person in an earthly business. When we fight our way to the top of what we refer to as success, we aim our attention at such achievement. A person who focuses their attention on achieving awareness of the totality of consciousness does not have too much interest in being a high achiever at an earthly level. They may be having a good job, but not something so strenuous that all energy goes into the achieving part. Their goal is to become aware of the creation's totality and assist other seekers ready for assistance. Their interest in an earthly income is only to allow their material body to live and work towards their goal.

When we live our lives entirely at the material level of awareness, we cannot recognise a person who is aware of higher awareness levels. We can look as much as we want, but we will pass the person we need and find a person who gives us the impression that they can provide us with what we require. We cannot recognise a real master; thus, we should not try. We can ask, and even that does not work. A real master will never tell us their capabilities; we either follow them or ignore them. To them, it is all the same.

The world always has people who are aware of the totality of their consciousness. These people are in places of the world where they are needed, and they find those that need them. When we realise this, we know that searching is not the way; we wait until we meet such a person. Most seekers are entirely sure that they are ready to meet a master. Although they have put a lot of effort in, their preparation may not be sufficient. Only a real master knows how to distinguish between who is ready and who must wait.

In our busy and stressful society, we can buy ourselves anything we want. Often, when we can afford it, this is what we do. Spirituality does not work this way. The wealthy need to go through an identical procedure as the poor and uneducated. Khalil Gibran told us about this in one of his short stories.

I need to tell the story in my words; I read it years ago in a Dutch book. I am not able to find the original story on the web.

The Fool

One day a fool and a wise man were sitting under a tree enjoying the beautiful weather when God came down to earth to meet them.
The wise man greeted God humbly and said: 'God, when can I finally leave this cycle of birth and death and join with you forever?'
God looked at the wise man and told him, "you are a wise man, and you have done a lot of good. Only four more lives you have to go through."
The wise man was disappointed, but he – being very wise – accepted his faith.
Then the fool asked God, "God, when can I join you forever?"

God looked at the fool and asked him, "see how many leaves there are on this tree? That is the number of lives you have to live before joining me forever!"

The fool stood up and danced while shouting, "finally, I know for sure that, eventually, I can join my God forever!"

God looked with love at the dancing fool and told him, "my son, come with me; you can join me right now!"

I do not believe that Khalil Gibran meant to say that a master is a fool. The intention is to show that what we collect on earth, which includes wisdom and material knowledge, is not essential. When we aim to become aware of our consciousness's totality, the mind's activities to acquire assets and understanding have only value at the material level of our awareness. All other levels do not require such earthly acquisitions.

Any person who reaches the perfection level that allows them to know how to access all awareness levels will be a master to a lay audience. However, the person them-self does not consider this achievement as special. There is still a long way to go before awareness of the nameless becomes a reality. Even when we are aware of our consciousness's totality, we are still part of a personality. To become aware of the nameless, we need to shed the last bit of the mind and the ego: no more desires and no more awareness of being a person. We are not a part of any personality at this awareness level. Our awareness dives into something that, to all intents and purposes, is "Nothing".

At this awareness level, we are everywhere and know every part of the creation. However, we still have our material body. How to live with such awareness? Only those that achieve this feat understand what it means.

Their task is to guide humanity to total awareness. The possibility exists that they may fail. Not to worry, other beings will come up at the material awareness level. A lot of entities reached total awareness, and more will achieve this level. Some perish in the folding's of time; others succeed.

Is there a purpose to this process? The term purpose is only valid at the material level of awareness, and humans only use it. In our world, we do not know of any entity that used the concept of purpose. It is a creation of the mind, and, eventually, it becomes of no concern when we leave the mind behind.

The whole task of the masters is to create awareness of the ultimate destination. We can, of course, deny that this is our goal. Those that guide us to this destination do not mind. Their task is to assist those who are ready. They wait for any entity that wants to follow the path. Until people want to reach total awareness, they can enjoy their life at the material awareness level. It is the task of every single person to declare to be ready. The master will never deny assistance to those that honestly wish to progress. Again, no stops are in place and no rules that only individually chosen souls can progress; it is entirely up to us. We are the sole controllers of our destiny.

-oOo-

We need to address one more subject: Who can assume the task as a master? We dealt with this above, so why do I create this question?

The number of people who can access the totality of their consciousness is severely limited, to the extent that there are no sufficient people like this to assist all that require assistance in this world. However, some seekers become disciples of such masters, and some seekers work alone but have a connection with a master. These people can and will assist others who need assistance.

Most seekers who ask for assistance require a person who can guide them in life's activities. They are on the path to spiritual awareness, but their progress is not such that they need a real master to bring them to the final awareness level. Another seeker can easily assist such people.

Some seekers can give initiation, and some can even access the totality of consciousness. These people can assist anybody who requires assistance. The art is to find such people; as we start meddling in the material world of spiritual help, we likely find those that are in there for the sole purpose of collecting material assets.

The decision of who to select as your master is solely up to you. Take such a decision but remember all that I explained. It will assist you on the way to your destination.

-oOo-

The Nameless

This chapter deals with the final step to merge in what we call: The Nameless.

After a lot of work, likely spending many lives at the material level of awareness, we finally cleaned our soul sufficiently to get to the phase that we are willing to off-load all our baggage and merge into our final destination. We raise our awareness level to enter the nameless.

Before I complete the story by discussing the concept of the nameless, I like to convey the following message:

Try to understand what I say and find another explanation. There is always a different way of bringing the story. When using a language at the material level of awareness, it is impossible to understand and describe reality. The idea behind writing this book is to assist those that follow the spiritual path. However, they should do so with a curious and open mind. I do not want people to take on my way of thinking; we are all unique; we should also develop our unique way of thinking.

Please understand that I wrote this book in 2021. Give it a few years, and my thinking will change like it does all the time. Ask me tomorrow, and I may tell a different story. Like life, my thinking changes. There is no continuity when following the spiritual path. The word "seeker" can, therefore, never be defined precisely. What we "seek" today may not be what we "seek" tomorrow.

-o0o-

Recently, I read that two well-known masters explained to somebody that going beyond the purely spiritual was frightening and dangerous. They did not want to discuss the matter, and they advised never to attempt this path.

The story made me change the drawing of consciousness and some of the explanations in this book. Why, if we look for the nameless, would those on the path refer to this in such terms? I realised that to go this way; we need to be capable of shedding our desires and the ego. These are difficult things to do. Our upbringing tells us who we are, and to get rid of this thought goes with the uncomfortable feeling that we lose ourselves.

Is it seriously frightening and dangerous to merge in the nameless? I do not believe it is. We originate from there; it is our true home. We may call our true home the purely spiritual, but we still appear to possess knowledge of who we are at that level of our consciousness. The meaning of this conclusion is that we still have an ego and, therefore, a connection with the mind.

Years ago, I used to tell people the story of life, and the ways to live this as follows:

> A group of people live in a small village.
> A river flows by the village; we do not know where the water goes.
> Most of us do not give this a thought; we go about our daily routines.
> Some of us sit by the river and wonder to what location the water flows.

Even fewer of us like to know more. We build a boat and float out, but we tie the boat with a rope to the shore.

Sometimes, a person is brave enough and cuts the rope and disappears forever.

The objective is to show that those who follow the spiritual path are a tiny minority of the population. Although many seekers follow the spiritual path, to wish to disappear is not something for the fainthearted. Why do this at all? I will try to explain where we go and what we encounter when taking this step.

-oOo-

When we refer to the nameless, we may also regard this as a substance in such a balanced state that the only way to understand the concept is to compare it with "Nothing". All that we – being humans at the material level of awareness – can understand is energy in some form of movement. As soon as the motion stops and the balance of everything we can measure amounts to zero, our comprehension disappears. We enter an awareness level that, to all intents and purposes, must be referred to as "Nothing". Time in this state also does not exist. All that we know is awareness and intelligence, while we feel nothing but love and devotion.

The terms awareness, intelligence, love and devotion as we know them at the material level of existence are not comparable with the feelings we have in this state. Although they are there, they are devoid of any attachment. When we show any sign of these feelings as we do at the physical level, we move out of this substance and continue our existence somewhere on the ladder of awareness of consciousness. We do not get kicked out; we remove ourselves.

Likely, the process is continuous.

A soul creates feelings of attachment, and it loses its connection with the nameless to continue its existence somewhere in our consciousness. When the feelings created are strong, the soul enters the material level of awareness. The nameless is in constant balance; nothing can disturb this. The open space between energy particles – as explained by our scientists – is this balanced energy.

I tried in a previous book to show how this sequence works via the use of a drawing:

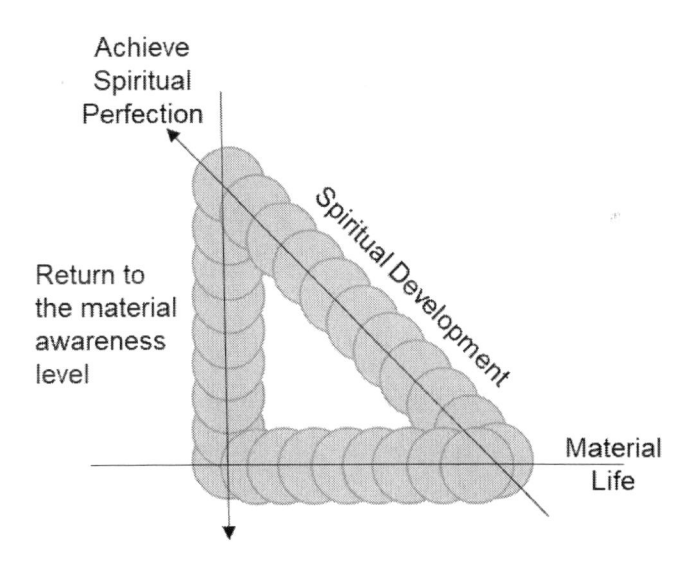

```
        Achieve
        Spiritual
       Perfection
            ↑
            |         Spiritual Development
            |
Return to   |
the material|
awareness   |
level       |
            |_____ Material
                                        Life
            ↓
```

The circles represent single lives. We live at the material level of awareness, but some take the step to climb out of this life. We keep on climbing until we reach the nameless, but we automatically move out and start again when we show any attachment or desire.

To give a simplistic example of such a state:

> When we put three balanced phases of generated electricity together in a cable, the result is that we do not measure an electrical field. The balance outside the cable, when the loading is even, will be zero. We may think that there is no electricity, but we can measure a field again when we separate the three phases. I do not want to suggest touching the wires, as it will prove the existence of energy in a very profound way. The concept of "Nothing" works like this.

As we raise our awareness to this level, we enter something that contains everything, while it also is perfectly balanced. Everything in existence is in this location, while the balancing causes it to be precisely zero. At last, we achieved entering "Nothing". We know all there is to know, and we are everywhere.

When we made adequate preparations via offloading our body of all the baggage, we enter this awareness phase and start again upon passing away. From nothing, the audible lifestream creates all the life forms and personalities. We purified ourselves to enter the nameless; we can now enter the cycle of life again but in a fully conscious state. We can choose to stay, or we can choose to go to higher levels of awareness. Nobody tells us what to do; it is our choice.

We can refer to a human who reached this state of awareness as a complete human. In my view, such a reference is better than the present terminology, which is a perfect living master. Whatever state of awareness we reach, we are still human. Possibly better, but I have my doubts. Our design is that of a hunter with sufficient intelligence to beat all other hunters in this material world. It will take a lot more than creating the ultimate awareness to get this design out of the system. Will it mean that no human can ever reach the phase of total awareness? I know it is possible because I met people who are. Can the whole of humanity raise itself to become complete humans? We know that more civilisations of humanoid status have been at the material level of awareness. They disappeared, to where we do not know. Let us hope that this means that our present civilisation can achieve the same.

The preceding version of the trajectory of life shows a line of thinking. We move via the outer path, go on via the inner route, and follow the spiritual domain's trajectory all the way to the final destination. When we arrive at this goal, we enter the nameless concept in a wholly purified state and become part of the story at the beginning.

All this may sound difficult to understand, and I agree that comprehending it is not easy. Why execute a lot of work, spread out over many lifetimes, and starting all over again? It is like running around in circles!

To me, we are part of a sequence with the objective to keep life going. We cannot step out of this series of events. As time is not a factor, we may think we are in a sequence and follow a path, but we only try to understand what we cannot comprehend at our awareness level. We are part of some form of a never-ending story. We do not need to comprehend what it is or why it happens because we do not move out. We accept it all and let life flow as it does.

-o0o-

As we are humans, we always like to look at the purpose of it all. Of course, we created this story based on information from various lines of thought, with some amendments and changes to relate what goes on to energy in vibration. The Western way of thinking does not usually involve many deities; thus, we left them out and created the sum of personalities. Merging in the totality of everything in existence may seem useless to some, but it is what those that practise real meditation aspire.

Time and other dimensions are all part of the illusions created by the mind. We do not know where we are and what we are. We do not understand why it all happens, and the story I created is one way of making sense of everything. We start the cycle of life from material to the nameless. We philosophise more and pose the possibility of many such processes, each separate and each part of a whole.

This whole will be the overarching totality of every creation. We can keep on philosophising about what goes on in our lives and the universe. However, to find out what really goes on, we need to follow our destination's spiritual path. Only when we reach our final goal will we know what else there is to do. Never assume that there is such a thing as a final goal. It does not exist; we can always go on.

To give those that intend to follow the spiritual path a bit of guidance, I added a chapter on meditation to this book. However, the best thing to do is live happy and unconcerned about what happens to us. Whatever happens, is part of a master plan. We are just a tiny spec in the creation, and although we can become part of the larger pieces, eventually it all comes down to going nowhere; we move our awareness into "Nothing".

-o0o-

The art of Meditation

When we practice meditation to follow the spiritual path, we need to go in two steps. This chapter gives a short description of what this entails.

Step 1 - Disciplining the Mind

In this step, we learn the art of disciplining our mind. The objective is to realise that we always engage the mind in a thinking process, which, when we analyse it, does not serve many purposes. Of course, we can accept what goes on and keep on living our lives as we did up to now, but in that case, we would not have picked up this book. The process to discipline the mind can take a while. Ideally, we should get this education from a very young age onward, but this did not happen. Expect that the process may take years and can never be a complete success. Do not see apparent failure as bad; any learning process takes time, and evaluating progress is very difficult. I tend to tell people that the difference between knowing a little bit and knowing a bit more is tough to detect. Part of discipline is to accept what goes on. When we move slow, so be it; whatever speed we progress will lead us, eventually, to the finish line.

-o0o-

From the start of our lives, others encourage us to direct our attention in thousands of directions. The Western cultural and behavioural way of life is to instruct a newly born to concentrate on outside subjects and completely forget that the real you is on the path inside of the body. Look at the world. People do their utmost to look good and different from others. From the start, people make us believe that we must copy role models. Following our intuition as a guide to behaving ourselves is not encouraged. Our mentors base this habit on the premise that the outside world is real.

To achieve a state of our mind that allows us to become aware of ourselves, we need to exercise control. Most people believe that the mind is who they are; they think continuously, and often their thoughts are repetitive. The mind, in that case, keeps itself busy; it proves it needs to exist. By exercising disciple over the process of thinking, we bring control over this thought process. We need to come to the phase that we use our mind as a tool. The mind is a very sophisticated tool, but it is a tool. It can help us live in this physical existence, but it is not an entity on its own.

The human consciousness is a complex entity, which exists over a range of awareness levels. The body is a part of this complex system, but it exists only at the physical awareness levels. The mind works at the physical awareness levels, but its influence reduces after the causal level. When we try to access the awareness levels above the causal level, we seriously reduce the mind's impact. We call the procedure to depart from the use of the mind "To die while living".

The world knows many ways to discipline the mind, and there are plenty of qualified teachers around. All these systems are acceptable, provided they suit you. As an older person, I cannot execute the exercises required for some of these systems. Do not worry; the procedure I provide works as well and does not require complicated gymnastic movements. Chose a design that you like, and work it to create the discipline required. Study what I provide for you below, and skip the parts you do differently.

We can execute the first three steps simultaneously. Do not underestimate what needs doing; it took me the best part of five years to get to a phase that I knew I had control over my thinking. However, my thoughts can still wander off.

To execute meditation exercises, sit in a place that gives you peace, quiet, where we feel safe, and where we are alone. The objective is to get rid of stress, feelings of fear, and repetitive thoughts. The exercises below assist, but we need to be entirely at ease. A separate room is ideal; make sure we do not get disturbed. Good moments are when we come out of bed and when we go to sleep. Initially, it will not be easy to concentrate longer than five minutes. Meditating for a long time is not helpful when we are impatient. We do the work for as long as we can keep the mind under control. When we get bored, stop meditating. It is essential to execute the exercise daily; weekly for hours is a lot less valuable than five minutes daily.

The first step is to stop the process of repetitive thinking.
We should not underestimate this step; it sounds easy, but it takes a lot of effort to control our thinking process. What worked for me was exercise. When I swim, scuba dive, or play squash, I focus all my attention on the game, and repetitive thinking stops. What also works for me is driving and only concentrate on the environment; I do not allow thoughts to interrupt me. Even watching TV works, I observe my body during the advertising and focus on the watching, trying not to identify the sounds.

The second step is to contemplate on a single subject.
Anything that comes to mind we pick up, analyse why we think that, and decide whether to delete the subject or retain. Do this for everything that

starts occupying the mind. Again, it sounds easy, but it is difficult to hold on to this system when stressed or tired. A proven technique is to pray. When we read about famous religious people, they often pray a lot. Doing this achieves the same as repeating mantras; it causes the mind to stop repetitive thinking. Of course, repeating a sentence or a word is a typical example of repetitive thinking, but it is different. A process like this will calm the mind, while repetitive thinking tends to cause stress. Besides, the process of repeating thoughts causes us to stray with our perception all around the world, while repeating mantras does the opposite; it focuses the mind.

The third step is to accept that we are not the mind.
We need a way to accept this and exercise control. To achieve this aim, we sit down and put our attention on the third eye. We do this as follows:

We think about a place between our ears, slightly above the centre point between our eyes. Doing this puts our attention on the pineal gland.

The spiritual literature tells us that the location of our soul is at this centre. I have a different opinion. Our soul is everywhere in the body. The body, however, is purely physical, while the soul is entirely spiritual. What the body requires is an interface between the soul and itself. This interface is the mind. When we learn to keep our attention focused on the pineal gland, we learn to separate the body from the soul in a particular way; we recognise that they are separate. We can compare this with knowing that we have individual parts of our body, like arms and legs. We also concentrate the soul at the third eye: we move our attention from everywhere to a single spot.

The first time we attempt these exercises, we likely find that we can focus our attention only for a few seconds. Our mind will wander off to all sorts of thoughts. It will take quite some time before we will be able to keep our attention concentrated on the pineal gland for a prolonged period. Please do not get discouraged by this; we had no education on this art; now we need to learn when we are adults. Exercise regularly, and at some stage, we find that our attention focuses automatically on the third eye.

Whatever we do as of now, we try to maintain our attention on this spot

In the early stages of meditation, I liked driving to work while maintaining my attention on the third eye and attempting to stop the process of thinking. There are many ways to train our mind to stop thinking and concentrate on this single point. Several exercises that are around are called forms of meditation. Use these; they are good exercises. However, be aware that the objective is to discipline the mind. During this process, we also find that we learn to avoid stress and the feeling of panic. These feelings are part of what the mind creates to prove its existence is essential. By learning to control the mind, we learn to overcome such feelings.

We now attempt to watch our body from this point

We become the audience; we observe what happens, but we try not to participate. Of course, now meditation becomes part of our everyday life. We work, we watch TV, and whatever else we do, we keep our attention on the third eye. We know that our lives consist of manipulations, short stories that create a reaction from us. To get ready for this acceptance, we need to create a feeling of separation. We look at the body and recognise that it is not what we are. We are the audience watching a theatre show, the theatre of life. Initially, doing this is difficult, as the mind keeps interfering and wandering off to other thoughts. However, after some time, it happens automatically.

The feeling that we are separate from our body is natural but not correct. We are not next to the body, but we know that the body exists; the body is not us. Some of us may comment that we create illusions and try to convince ourselves that these are real. I agree that we create illusions, but do not forget that this whole world is an illusion. As long as we realise that we live in an environment that is a creation, it is not real; we can just as well add another illusion to our perception.

The objective of the illusion is to create a feeling that makes our attention go inward

The pineal gland is the location that allows us to see the path inward. For now, we work on discipline, but during this process, we recognise the road that needs following, which is the inner path.

Redirecting our attention to the inner path is not easy. We need to change our focus from the physical domain, governed by time, to an environment without restrictions. When making this step, we lose the perception created by our senses. There is no easy way to make this jump; we need pulling from the physical reality to the soul's existence.

The objective of creating discipline is to render our body and mind ready for this step. Although we say that the mind holds us back, this statement only refers to our inability to control the mind as a tool. When we master the control required, the mind becomes our ally; all physical parts of our existence work to the goal of achieving awareness of the domains of the soul.

-oOo-

Step 2 - Real Meditation

All the exercises we did up to now mean to discipline the mind and teach us to keep our thinking process under control. Without doing this, we will not be able to follow the concentration process that we refer to as real meditation. We now move to learn about this way of meditating.

Again a warning; everything in life is about us following our unique path to spiritual learning. I provide a way to achieve this, but it follows my path. It is not wrong to learn from this book, but the objective is to develop your method. I still listen to those who, in my view, are competent to know how to proceed, but I also make up my mind. Strange enough, I concluded some far-reaching realities while, at a later stage, finding write-ups from masters who tell similar stories. Of course, these stories were available already, but I needed to progress to the phase that I was ready to find them. Before that, I likely read the words, but the reality behind them escaped me. Be aware of this issue; it is part of the process of realisation.

-oOo-

Why do I call this system "real meditation"?

Most of the meditation exercises available worldwide are very useful to discipline the mind and cure some of the mental issues we experience. However, they do not assist us in finding and exploring higher levels of awareness. All these exercises are called meditation, and often the practitioners tell us that their system is superior. Some courses teach us that we should concentrate on the main seven chakras in our body, as this exercise gives us wonderful spiritual experiences.

I do not want to go in the direction of ranking meditation systems based on suitability. All exercises are suitable to follow, but primarily they relate to the body and the physical levels of our existence. To go further to the soul's awareness levels, we need to practice systems designed for this path. Some exist, and when a person is ready for this step, they will search for it and find what they require. Most of us need assistance to move past the physical levels of awareness. The move is not simple; often, it gets compared with a jump into the unknown. When we are ready for this move, assistance comes to us in the form of an outside master. Such a person assists by connecting us to the inner guide, who is the real master, and who shows us the way.

Do not actively search for a master, as we will find somebody. However, this person is most likely suitably qualified and knowledgeable but firmly immersed in the material awareness level. This issue becomes apparent when all assistance comes at a cost. Proper spiritual help does not relate to the material awareness level and should not come for a price. The aid we require will arrive via a person who becomes our friend. Accept the format, and do not insist on being shown the way. Actual progress happens when we are ready. As long as we demand to receive initiation by the master, we work along a path that belongs at the material level of awareness; we are not ready. Learn to accept that patience is a virtue, and all will go well.

-o0o-

Real meditation has the objective of exploring the awareness of the various levels of our consciousness; with the result that we raise our understanding, so we experience more aspects of our being. Initially, we do this via meditation and our awareness experiences various parts of our being. The first step is that we experience all aspects of our senses without the body. Those who study spirituality refer to this state as the astral plane. It is not a different location or a different world; it is another aspect of what we are. After further concentration, we can achieve reaching the domain of our mind, the causal plane.

Both planes are part of what constitutes our mind, and some masters even refer to the characteristics of us that reach these planes as separate bodies. The comparison with bodies is logical, as these planes constitute the outer path. Anything to do with the mind is caught in the dimension of time and relates to the physical bodies. Statements that in the astral plane, we can travel at lightning speed to other galaxies are correct. However, it indicates that we are limited to the bondage of time and the dimensions going with this factor.

Raising our awareness past the mind's domain requires us to move from our physical bodies to an awareness level controlled by very different laws and does not adhere to the dimension of time. There is no easy way of going to this level of awareness. We need to leave all that is familiar to us, everything that we know and can understand. Anything we learnt after our birth needs to go; we dive into the unknown. Spiritual literature refers to this step as: "To die while being alive". The way to progress is with the assistance of somebody who went past this barrier before. The person goes first and pulls the disciple along via the use of a feeling. We call this feeling "love".

Although it appears relatively straightforward, it is not, as creating this feeling does not relate to what we understand it to be. The term love at the material level of awareness has a lot of conditions attached to it. A change of the original requirements can change the feeling. Real love – as used by a master – is not conditional; it is, therefore, permanent. To create such a feeling, we need to work very hard at our mindset; no judging, no conditions, just love. We can start by identifying the feeling by comparing it to someone or something we love. After the identification, we need to hold on to this feeling unconditionally. We can only do this after we have mastered control over the five vices.

How do we execute real meditation?

Up to now, we meditated at specific moments, sitting down in a particular place. When we advance further, we should focus on the third eye all the time, whatever we do. Keep the focus during the day. It is commendable to have a short meditation exercise in the morning and the evening, but it is more important to keep the focus on the third eye going as much as we can during the day.

We find that this exercise becomes the norm after a few weeks. During any activity, we will experience a kind of separation. We are at the third eye centre, and our body executes whatever work we do. We may also experience the feeling of being a separate body from our material body, but larger. What we experience is the astral body.

Another experience we get is a feeling of love. Initially, this feeling is faint, and one thinks that those that describe it are making something small look enormous. We also feel that the exercise is superfluous; why are people making it look like we get fantastic experiences? Later on, we start looking for the feeling. It is still faint, and we notice that it disappears when we fall back to ordinary thoughts. We only experience it when we manage to still the mind. Keep working on this, and suddenly we realise that we want to have the experience again. We now have the guide that pulls us towards the domain of the soul.

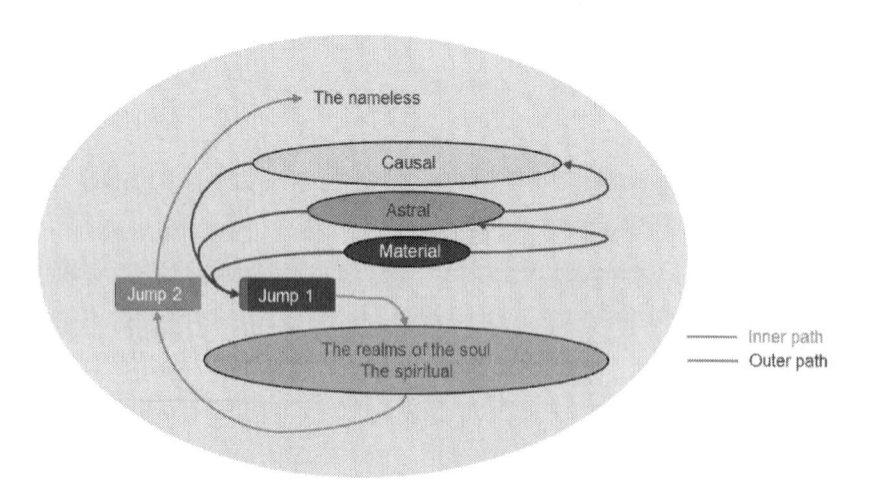

I will use the above figure, which I used before. The drawing shows that we can follow the traditional route from the material domain via astral to causal. However, at any moment, we can make the jump to the realm of the soul. Going directly to the nameless may be possible, but it means that we rid ourselves of our ego at a very early stage. There are too many chains tying us to the material level of consciousness to recommend skipping all steps, provided that this is possible.

The second jump to the nameless is a lot more challenging than the first jump. The spiritual literature I studied explains little about this jump. From what I see, it is a very complex thing to achieve. Can it be one while we still occupy the material body? I do not know.

Most of those who follow the spiritual path love the astral level's experiences; they do not want to proceed any further. A few on the way, move on to the causal level, and that is the end. To pass on, we need to make the jump to the level of the soul. Can this be done without assistance? The story is that some people achieved this feat. We cannot verify this, and mainly we discuss now people like Buddha and Krishna. Their followers make these statements, but they likely met others when they went into solitary confinement. We cannot be sure. The best is to work on the exercises described in this book and become patient. Our inner guide will ensure that we receive what is required and when it needs doing.

Requiring anything to be done fast and with a minimum of effort is a typical expectation of the present-day Western culture. Try not to fall for this way of living. We can avoid a lot of effort by paying other people to do the work, but we can only do this at the material level of awareness. Spiritual progress we make alone, we cannot skip steps at a price, and we cannot hire other people to do the work for us. Get used to being the worker; become a seeker.

-o0o-

References

The Path of the Masters by Julian Johnson

U-tube lectures by Ishwar Puri

Anatomy of Consciousness by Ishwar Puri

Various stories by Khalil Gibran

Various Poems by Rumi

The Alternative by Marcel van Heijzen

Study books by Cyndy Dale

About the author

Marcel started his adult working life as an electrical engineer. He has been working as an engineer and project manager in various parts of the world.

Nearing the end of his working life, he got diagnosed with level four prostate cancer. His oncologist informed him that he had around four months to live. It was at this moment that he met a person who knew how to cure this terminal disease.

After this challenge, Marcel committed to assisting others who go through a terminal disease. Marcel does this by writing books about spirituality, running a website that deals with spirituality and writing regular blogs, aiming to assist people who have contracted a severe disease and people who are consciously starting on the path of spirituality.

You can reach Marcel as follows:

Marcel.vanheijzen@yahoo.co.uk
https://alyaconsultancy.com/

About this book

A friend asked me a question that led to defining the concept of Nothing. I gave this a thought and felt that it was time to address spiritual realities, which do not exist in ordinary people's eyes. They are equivalent to Nothing.

During the writing of this book, I had a lot of assistance. The names of those assisting me are in the section of acknowledgements.

This book adds a lot of background to the previous book I wrote, The Alternative. The writing is kept concise and to the point; I avoided lengthy explanations to fill pages.

Enjoy the reading, and try to find your way on the path to discover the secrets of our consciousness.

Meditation is not something that separates people from life; it is part of life itself, and it assists those that learn this art to lead a healthy and fulfilling lifestyle.

Printed in Great Britain
by Amazon